AM I DOING THIS RIGHT?

GOD'S DESIGN FOR RELATIONSHIPS THAT LAST

GREG LAURIE

CONTRIBUTIONS FROM JONATHAN LAURIE

AM I DOING THIS RIGHT?

GOD'S DESIGN FOR RELATIONSHIPS THAT LAST

GREG LAURIE

CONTRIBUTIONS FROM JONATHAN LAURIE

AM I DOING THIS RIGHT?

CONTENTS

INTRODUCTION
Is There a Right Way of Doing This?

"Two people are better off than one,
for they can help each other succeed."
—Ecclesiastes 4:9 (NLT)

By God's grace, I've had the privilege of being married to my wife, Cathe, for 52 years now. I guess you could say we've been around the sun enough times to know a few things about relationships. But one thing we know for sure: God designed relationships for our good and for His glory. He designed them to last.

If you look at our culture, you see a different story.

Despite a positive trend over the last decade, roughly 42 percent of marriages still end in divorce.[1]

Only 37 percent of adults ages 25–49 report living with spouses and children (that's down from 67 percent in 1970).[2]

What's more, although most young people say that they want a romantic relationship, over 90 percent believe that dating is harder than ever before.[3] More and more are putting off marriage until later in life. Predictably, the age at which people are getting married for the first time is at an all-time high.[4]

In a world where relationships seemingly fail to live up to their promises, the common question is, *"Am I doing this right?"*

The church has a unique opportunity to equip people with hope, help, and practical tools for every relationship. Younger audiences, in particular, are hungry for real-life advice on friendship, dating, marriage, and intimacy. Throughout these pages, I provide answers by drawing from Scripture, sharing insights from my son Jonathan, and offering practical applications to help your relationships not only survive—but thrive.

While marriage is a key focus, emphasizing God's design for covenant and commitment, this book speaks to every season of life. Whether you're single and seeking purpose, dating with marriage in mind, cultivating true friendships, or bravely sharing your faith, these chapters will guide you toward healthy connections that last.

Remember, it was God who created us to live in unity, and nobody knows better than He does about how relationships are supposed to function. For this reason, we must learn the strong principles given to us in Scripture and follow them with all our hearts. We must come together as friends, families, and the church to cultivate purpose and lasting commitment. We must pass on legacies that glorify God, edify the church, and evangelize the world.

The Bible speaks to every generation. Its principles are every bit as true and relevant as they were a hundred, or even a thousand years ago. It's these enduring principles we will explore together in this book. Each chapter is followed by prayer and thought-provoking questions for reflection and discussion. It is my hope that you'll share this resource with your friends, neighbors, and small groups, inviting them to discover God's design for lasting relationships.

From the start, however, you'll need strength beyond your own. If you truly want this book to be a real force in your life and relationships, I suggest you do this: Set the book down for a few moments and ask God's Holy Spirit to speak. Ask Him to teach you, strengthen you, and enable you with power beyond your own. And remember:

You are not in this alone. You can trust God's design.

You can form relationships that last.

Marriage Is God's Idea

"And the LORD *God said, 'It is not good that man should be alone; I will make him a helper comparable to him.'"*
—Genesis 2:18 (NKJV)

My friend James Merritt says, "If you're in a bad marriage, it's not because God had a bad idea. Marriage is His ideal idea. The problem is we get married, and we turn an ideal into an ordeal, and then we want to look for a *new* deal."

The truth is, we either believe God's idea is good, or we don't. In 2 Timothy 3:16, the apostle Paul said, "All Scripture is God-breathed and is useful for teaching, rebuking, correcting and training in righteousness" (NIV).

As Christians, this is the biblical worldview that we're called to have, so what happens when we look at something in our life and realize, *this doesn't line up with what the Bible has to say?* Our view on dating, marriage, sexual immorality, or anything else . . . what happens when it doesn't line up with God's view? Well, we should fix it!

What do you do when you come to a verse in the Bible you disagree with? You change your opinion. And when it comes to God's idea of marriage, we change our opinion because we believe that the Bible is absolute truth. It is God's Word. It's His eternal, timeless values that are true yesterday, today and forever.

Almost everything in our society, our view of singleness, dating, marriage, etc., is either influenced by godly principles or completely tainted by the world. And with as outspoken as the culture is, it's easy to get away from God's original plan. But remember, the Bible begins with a wedding in the book of Genesis and ends with a wedding when the bride (the church) and Bride Groom (Christ) are joined together. From beginning to end, marriage is God's idea.

Modeling Our Role Models

This first marriage of Adam and Eve is effectively a model for every marriage. In the second chapter of Genesis, the Bible tells the story of how "the LORD God caused the man to fall into a deep sleep. While the man slept, the LORD God took out one of the man's ribs and closed up the opening. Then the LORD God made a woman from the rib, and he brought her to the man" (verses 21–22 NLT).

When Adam first saw Eve, his thoughts probably went like this: "Yes! This is good! She's amazing!" But here's what Adam really said in Genesis 2:23: "This one is bone from my bone, and flesh from my flesh! She will be called 'woman,' because she was taken from 'man'" (NLT).

Eve was perfect in every way for Adam. At last, Adam had a partner, someone with whom he could share his life, his thoughts, and his joys. (He didn't have any concerns or worries to share at that point.)

Why does the Bible say God "brought" Eve to Adam? This is a very important question to answer. Why does He bring us together as men and women? The answer is in Genesis 2:18: "I will make him a helper comparable to him" (NKJV). The Hebrew word for *helper* can be translated to mean "someone who assists another to reach fulfillment." It was used elsewhere in the Old Testament in reference to someone coming to the rescue of another.

So, Eve, in a very real sense, came to rescue Adam from his loneliness. God says that she is "comparable" to Adam, or corresponding to him. This is important because we live in a time and a culture that seeks to blur the differences between men and women. The assertion is that if certain social conditioning factors were changed, we would find that men and women are really the same. But that simply isn't true.

Unblurring the Lines

After a huge and involved social experimentation in the 1960s and '70s, researchers finally concluded that boys are boys and girls are girls. (I could have told them that and saved all that time and money.) If we fail to recognize—and appreciate—this basic reality, we're being very foolish. It doesn't mean that one gender is better than the other. Men are not better than women, and women are not better than men. No, they are *different*. And both have been uniquely created in God's image.

In his book *Love for a Lifetime*, Dr. James Dobson cites some of the physiological differences between men and women. He points out that men and women differ in every cell of their body. For instance, a woman has greater constitutional vitality because of the chromosome difference. She usually outlives a man by three or four years, and in some cases, much longer. They also differ in their metabolism. Women have slower metabolisms than men, and different skeletal structures.[5]

We are different, and God *made* us that way. It's all a part of our Creator's good and wise plan.

Yoking Equally

Another super important part of God's design for marriage is mentioned in 2 Corinthians 6:14, saying, "Do not be unequally yoked with unbelievers. For what partnership has righteousness with lawlessness? Or what fellowship has light with darkness?" (ESV).

"To be yoked" is a phrase that is lost today, especially on us who are not farmers. Now some of you may be farmers, and that's awesome. We love you. We need farmers. But for those of us who aren't, a yoke is a piece of wood that literally straps two animals together. Think of two oxen from that old *Oregon Trail* game. You remember that old computer game, right? The one where Betsy died of typhus?

Anyway, when two animals are tied together, you don't want them to be unequally yoked (such as a living ox and a dead ox). In that case, the strong, healthy ox begins to drag the other one, but only for so long. Eventually, he's going to get pulled in the direction of the dead animal. So, if we are unequally yoked, as a believer and a nonbeliever, we're going to get pulled in the direction of the weaker one, right? That's why Paul made it clear not to be unequally yoked with nonbelievers.

Undermining God's Design

Marriage was God's idea before He created the church, the state, the school, or any of these things. His design for marriage came first, and that tells us something. It tells us that marriage is the very foundation of the family, and the family is the very foundation of the nation. As marriage goes, so goes the family. As the family goes, so goes the nation.

Long before there was a nation, a government, a school, or even a church, there was a man and a woman brought together to be husband and wife. The institution of marriage predates every other human institution or relationship in Scripture, and remains one of the key foundation stones of any society.

That is why our nation is in so much trouble right now—because of the breakdown of the family. And why is there a breakdown in the family? Because Satan hates what God loves. God loves us. He created marriage for us. Satan, knowing the power of marriage and the strength of the family in a nation, has done everything he can to undermine them.

It's worth noting that the devil doesn't even enter the scene until Eve is created. I'm not blaming it on Eve, but I'm saying as soon as a man and a woman come together, the devil steps right in goes, "Okay, we've got to put a stop to this. We can't have unity in this relationship." That's when the attacks begin.

God brought Adam and Eve together and established marriage with the immortal words: "Therefore shall a man leave his father and his mother, and shall cleave unto his wife: and they shall be one flesh" (Genesis 2:24 KJV).

It's interesting to note that Jesus quotes this statement in the New Testament. The Pharisees came to Him and asked, "Is it lawful for a man to divorce his wife for just any reason?" (Matthew 19:3 NKJV).

Quoting from Genesis, Jesus replied, "Have you not read that He who made them at the beginning 'made them male and female,' and said, 'For this reason a man shall leave his father and mother and be joined to his wife, and the two shall become one flesh'?" (Matthew 19:4–5 NKJV).

Genesis 2:24 provides some essential truths regarding God's design for marriage. In fact, two words sum it up: *leave* and *cleave*. First you must leave. Then you must cleave.

Pack Your Suitcase: It's Time to Leave

Marriage begins with leaving—a distinct departure and distancing from all other relationships. The closest relationship outside of marriage is specified here, which is the relationship of a child to his parents. This implies that, if it's necessary to leave your father and mother, then all lesser ties must be broken, changed, or left behind. You leave all other relationships.

Yes, you are still a son or a daughter to your parents, but it is different now because you have been joined to your spouse. Your relationship with your parents has changed. A new family has been established. Once he is married, the man's primary commitment is to his wife, and her primary commitment is to him.

Sadly, what happens in many marriages is that this vital process of leaving never takes place. One or both parties think, "If things don't work out, I'll go home to Mommy." Or maybe, "If things don't work out, I'll go back to my old friends and hang out with them." People who think this way have never really left other relationships, and haven't chosen to cleave to their spouse.

You need to learn to work things out as husband and wife. You need to learn how to communicate. And yes, you need to learn how to *disagree*. During my initial premarital counseling session with a couple, I will ask, "Have you two had a fight yet?" (Not a fistfight, but a disagreement.)

"No," some reply. "We *never* argue."

And then I'll surprise them and say, "Okay, you need to get out of here then, because I'm not going to marry you. Go have a few arguments, and then we can talk."

The fact is you have to learn how to agreeably disagree. You have to learn what to do in situations where you don't see eye to eye. You need to know how to wrestle with an issue as a couple, how to resolve your differences, and how to forgive one another. Without learning these vital lessons, you are in danger of turning every disagreement into a battle, and you'll begin to resent each other.

If you are a husband, your best friend and closest confidant needs to be your wife. If you are a wife, the same needs to be true of your husband. It's good to have other friends, but there should only be one best friend in your life, and it should be your spouse.

It becomes especially dangerous when a wife has male friends other than her husband, and a husband has female friends other than his wife. Whether we will it or not, we begin bonding with these people. Before you know it, this "innocent friendship" isn't quite so innocent anymore, and can lead into the devastation of adultery.

Most adulterous relationships, especially in the case of women, do not begin with sexual attraction. They begin because a woman feels her husband isn't giving her the attention she wants and isn't spending time with her. So, she develops a friendship with a man who shows some interest.

"Oh, we're just friends," she might explain. "It's nothing more. He understands me. I understand him. We encourage one another. We pray together. We read the Bible together."

But understand this: *It's not going to work.* May I repeat that? *It's not going to work.*

"We're just friends" will change into something else, and that change can happen more quickly than you might imagine.

The same goes for men. A man might say, "This lady at work—we really understand each other. We talk about everything. She's not my wife; she's my *work wife.*"

Watch out! Never underestimate the power of emotional and physical attraction between a man and a woman. Before you know it, you'll find yourself entangled in a relationship you never meant to get involved in.

Husbands, make your wife your best friend. Wives, make your husband your best friend. Cultivate the friendship in your marriage. After all, the very purpose of marriage from the beginning was companionship. Yes, sexual intimacy is a big and wonderful part of the equation—a way to express the oneness that exists between a man and a woman. But that aspect, too, ought to be built on friendship and warm companionship.

Those who have been in good marriages for many years will affirm the importance of companionship. And even those who have been widowed and later remarried will say, "It's so good to do things together like going to the grocery store, washing the car, just sitting together on the couch and watching an old movie, whatever. It's so good not to be alone anymore."

It's terribly sad to see friendship lost in a marriage. The husband and wife may be lovers, good parents to their children, and an efficient-working team getting through life's demands. But it is so very sad if they have forgotten what it means to be friends.

Sometimes you see a couple in a restaurant, eating in the same booth but never looking at or saying a word to each other. It's so obvious that the friendship has gone out of their relationship (if it was ever really there), and they simply have nothing to say to one another. How very sad. And lonely! Soon, that lack of friendship begins to affect everything else in the marriage, and they begin to drift apart.

Listen to what God says in Malachi 2:14: "The LORD has been witness between you and the wife of your youth, with whom you have dealt treacherously; yet she is your companion and your wife by covenant" (NKJV).

Note the words *companion* and *wife*. That word *companion* can be translated from the Hebrew to mean "one you are united with in thoughts, goals, plans, and efforts." God is saying that we should be unified with our spouse in thoughts, goals, plans, and efforts.

We must walk the talk and make a commitment to stand on God's Word—to stand on His truth. As companions, we make a sure covenant, write it out, and seal it. This is part of the "leaving" process. Then in 1 Peter 3, we read, "Husbands, likewise, dwell with them with understanding, giving honor to the wife, as to the weaker vessel, and as being heirs together of the grace of life, that your prayers may not be hindered" (verse 7 NKJV).

The word Peter used for *dwell* means "to be aligned to or to give maintenance to." So, to put it all together, we hear God saying, "Be aligned, and give maintenance to your wife. Be united with her in thoughts, goals, plans, and efforts."

We think nothing of maintaining our cars or our garden, but it comes as a shock to us that our marriage needs maintenance as well!

What happens if you never maintain a car?

It will break down.

What happens if you neglect your garden?

It will be overrun with weeds.

And what happens if you do not maintain your marriage?

It, too, will fall apart.

For this reason, I must periodically take stock of my life and ask myself if there is any relationship or pursuit that I'm involved in that would put distance between me and my mate. Is anything getting in the way of our closeness? Anything at all? My career, perhaps? My hobby? My obsession with this or that? Is there anything in my life that might be crowding or damaging my relationship with my spouse?

If there is, *take action*!

Friendship, companionship, and closeness form the foundation of marriage. Every other relationship in your life must work in proportion with the relationship between you and your spouse. Yes, there's a place for buddies. There's a place for hobbies. There's a place for involvement in church activities. There's a place for business. But you shouldn't let anything obstruct your relationship with your spouse. That is all a part of "leaving."

And then there's the second part of God's design: There must be a *cleaving*. It's no use leaving unless you are willing to spend a lifetime cleaving.

Unpack for Good: It's Time to Cleave

The very purpose of marriage in the beginning was *companionship*. The word used in Genesis 2:24 for *cleave* means "to adhere to, to stick to, to be attached by some strong tie." You may be thinking, "That's me, alright. I'm stuck."

But that's not what this word means. In the verb form, it speaks of something that is done aggressively—a determined action. It's actually the idea of holding onto something. That is, it's not that you're stuck to something like a fly in a web, trying to get free. This is something you deliberately grip and hold, hanging on for dear life.

The word *cleave* speaks of a determined action. If you were walking along a cliff, suddenly lost your footing, fell over the edge, and grabbed a branch as you fell, you would cleave to that branch because it's something you very much want to do! Why? Because your very life would depend on it.

That's the whole idea of the word *cleave* as used here. You and your spouse aren't holding onto each other passively but aggressively. You are not stuck together as much as you are sticking together. This is what needs to happen in our marriages. It's sometimes a slippery, stormy world out there, and we need to hang on to each other.

Let's face it, there are so many pressures that seek to pull a husband and wife apart these days. Staying together, then, needs to be a determined action. Imagine you're walking with your spouse up a steep hillside covered with slippery wet grass on a windy day. You'd hold onto each other, wouldn't you? In the same way, husbands and wives need to take deliberate action to cling to one another and to stay away from anything that might come between them. That's the idea here in the Hebrew language.

When you come to the New Testament use of the same word in the Greek language, it means "to cement together, to stick like glue, or to be welded together so the two cannot be separated without serious damage to both." Again, we must periodically ask ourselves if there are any relationships or pursuits that are putting distance between us. Is there anything driving us apart? If so, will it eventually tear our relationship down?

Keep in mind, it's not always the big things that bring a marriage down. Certainly, there are big problems such as unfaithfulness or abuse, that can destroy a marriage quickly. But it's the little things, over time, that often chip away at the relationship until it crumbles.

As Song of Solomon says, it's "the little foxes that spoil the vines" (2:15 NKJV).

In a marriage, it can be a matter of neglecting the principle of leaving and cleaving. When there is an unwillingness to hold on tightly to your spouse, your marriage can begin to weaken. Problems can develop. So, cleave to your spouse, recognizing that all other relationships must be secondary.

An integral part of this companionship is communication. I always make sure to communicate with my wife throughout the day. I call her up, or drop her an email or a text. I like to tell her what's going on and bring her up to speed, and she does the same for me. But here's what amazes me. Sometimes I'll relate a conversation or experience that happened to me at the office or on one of my trips. Then, maybe weeks later, I'll hear her describing my experience to someone else. She describes it so vividly and accurately that I ask myself, "Was she with me? No, she couldn't have been. How does she know all this?" The fact is, she just knows me. She knows what I mean when I say certain words. She reads things into the tone of my voice. We've been husband and wife for a long time, and we just *know* each other. All too often, however, a marriage will face a breakdown in communication. And unless those breaks are soon mended, it can begin to damage the relationship.

I heard about an elderly husband and wife who had been married for many years. They were sitting together at the breakfast table. In a sudden, impulsive burst of loving emotion, the husband said, "Honey, I'm so proud of you."

His wife, however, was hard of hearing, and had misplaced her hearing aids.

"What's that?" she said.

"Honey, I'm so proud of you."

"What's that?"

"Honey, I'm so PROUD of you."

"I can't hear you."

"Honey, I'M PROUD OF YOU."

"Well," she huffed, "I'm tired of you, too."

Yes, there are communication problems along the way, as there will be between any two human beings. But a man and a woman who have determined in their hearts to cleave together no matter what will find a way to rebuild every damaged bridge and reopen every blocked path. The truth is . . .

God will help us if we ask Him.

He wants us to leave and cleave even more than we do.

Cleaving Is Easy in Paradise

Eden was no myth or fairyland, but it was paradise. The Bible identifies it as an actual piece of real estate, and we're even given some GPS coordinates . . . well, something like that. Genesis 2:8 (NKJV) tells us, "The Lord God planted a garden eastward," locating it near the area of the present-day Tigris and Euphrates Rivers. If you had lived in that era, and could have had a computer with you, you could have located it on Google Earth.

We also read in Genesis 2:11 of places called Pishon and the "land of Havilah." While we don't know for certain where these places were, the fact that they are mentioned shows that these were actual geographical places.

The whole world must have been beautiful and lush before Adam and Eve's fall, but the Garden of Eden was something really special. Think of all of the gorgeous places you've ever seen—every vision of every tropical isle on every travel website. Eden surpassed all of those. Eden was perfection. It must have been easy for Adam and Eve to "cleave" in paradise. After all, there were no in-laws, financial hardships, or toddlers running around. In fact, they could have been models for the "Garden of Eden Travel Website" (excluding their nakedness, of course).

Jonathan's Story: Speaking of paradise, my wife, Brittni, and I just celebrated our 15-year anniversary. That's a pretty big deal, right? To celebrate, we got away for a couple of days to Palm Springs. Before lunch one day, we wanted to find a good little hike to go on, just a nice walk. As I was looking for places, I was like, "Where in the heck is a good walk in Palm Springs, somewhere that's not 120 degrees?" (For those of you outside the area, Palm Springs literally gets up to 120 degrees in the summer.)

It was only April, but it would reach at least 110 during the peak of the day. So, we set out early at 8:30 in the morning, and arrived at a randomly selected spot called "Tahquitz Canyon." Even though I couldn't pronounce it, I was blown away by the hike. It was one of the coolest things we've ever done.

The hike itself was super easy, which made it a plus. I think the whole thing was about two miles round trip. As we started off, there was a little creek running by, and lots of vegetation, making it a little bit cooler, which was nice. As we went on, the stream turned into a bigger, wider, deeper stream. I kept commenting, "How clear is this stream? This is amazing. All I've seen in Palm Springs are stagnant ponds and golf courses with fake water features." But when we finally got to the end, there was a 60-foot waterfall. I was blown away. Where in the world were we? It was not the Palm Springs we knew! It was a literal paradise.

As impressed as my wife and I were in our little unexpected paradise, it didn't compare to the Garden of Eden. It didn't even come close. According to Genesis 2:15 (NKJV), it was Adam's job to "tend and keep" that beautiful garden. This doesn't mean he was a glorified gardener, walking around clipping grass and trimming hedges. The Hebrew word used here for *keep* is a word that means "discover its secrets." And who can even imagine how many wonderful secrets God built into that wondrous garden?

You see, cleaving was easy in Paradise. Adam and Eve had a close relationship with God and each other. They had everything they could ever want or need. Until they were distracted by something they couldn't have. What should have been a blissful companionship with shared goals, dreams, and visions of the future, became a new reality of struggle.

To "leave and cleave" as the Bible instructs, it takes hard work. And that's what we'll talk about in the next chapter.

Prayer: Lord, would You reveal in us the truths about marriage that we have missed and the ways that others have influenced our beliefs? We have become more of what the culture, society, and television say, rather than what the Bible says. Lord, would You convict our hearts? Would You lead us back to Yourself? We don't want to be led astray from Your plan. Thank You for being incredibly patient with all of us. We want to stand on absolute truth, even when it's unpopular, even when it's difficult. We want to be able to stand before You, hearing the words of the master who said, "Well done, good and faithful servant; you were faithful over a few things, I will make you ruler over many things. Enter into the joy of your lord." God, that's what we want. In the name of Your Son, Jesus, amen.

QUESTIONS for Discussion

1. God said, "It is not good that man should be alone; I will make him a helper comparable to him" (Genesis 2:18 NKJV). What does this verse imply about the companionship God intended for a husband and wife from the very beginning?

2. *A helper comparable to him* could be translated from the Hebrew as "someone who assists another to reach fulfillment." List some of the ways we do that for one another in our marriages.

3. What do we do when our view of marriage doesn't line up with what the Bible has to say? How have you and your spouse handled differing views in the past? How can you change your beliefs to align with the authority of God's Word as mentioned in 2 Timothy 3:16?

4. The chapter states that the "institution of marriage predates every other human institution or relationship in Scripture." How has the importance—the primacy—of this institution been diminished or degraded by today's culture? How can we as believers reestablish the once-high position and value of marriage with the upcoming generations?

5. Read Genesis 2:24 (KJV). Describe the importance of "leaving" before "cleaving" in a marriage. What happens in a marriage when that leaving is only partial? What happens when couples don't cleave through difficult trials?

6. Why does Greg say he won't marry a couple until they've had their first big fight?

7. Why is it so important that your spouse should also be your best friend? What are some ways to really *cultivate* that friendship?

8. What are the dangers associated with husbands and wives not paying enough attention to one another?

9. People who have been widowed talk about missing doing the little things together like going to the grocery store, taking walks, preparing a meal, even doing the laundry. How can we gain a fresh perspective on the importance of just being with each other and "doing life" together?

10. Malachi 2:14 says: "The Lord has been a witness between you and the wife of your youth, with whom you have dealt treacherously; yet she is your companion and your wife by covenant" (NKJV). What does the covenant of marriage mean in this day and age? What does it mean to you?

11. The Hebrew word translated as *companion* means "one you are united with in thoughts, goals, plans, and efforts." To what extent do those words describe your relationship with your spouse? If you're not experiencing that sort of companionship in your marriage, what are some practical ways you can make progress in that direction?

12. The word *cleave* in marriage speaks of a determined action. It means you deliberately grip or hold on to your mate, not allowing posses-

sions, preoccupations, or other people to come between you. Why does this seem to be such a challenge to so many in today's world? How can you and your spouse regain this closeness if you sense you might be losing it?

CHAPTER 2

Why Love Takes Work

"Lead a life worthy of your calling, for you have been called by God. Always be humble and gentle. Be patient with each other, making allowance for each other's faults because of your love. Make every effort to keep yourselves united in the Spirit, binding yourselves together with peace."
—Ephesians 4:1–3 (NLT)

Sometimes, I hear people say they have "a marriage made in Heaven," which is a nice sentiment, but does that mean other people have a marriage made in Hell?

If you have a happy marriage, a strong marriage, "a marriage made in Heaven" so to speak, that's because you have applied yourself. On the other hand, if your marriage is hurting, that's probably because you've neglected things, and that's how it works. If you neglect something long enough, it eventually falls apart.

I've heard it said that marriage is like a three-ring circus: engagement ring, wedding ring, and suffering. Now I hope that's not the case for you! We want to do marriage right, and it takes work.

Personally, I've seen it done wrong far too many times. My mother was married and divorced seven times, and she had a bunch of boyfriends in between her husbands. As I watched my mom's life unfold, I knew it was not the life I wanted to live. But stats tell us that if you come from a divorced home, it's a far greater possibility that you, yourself, will end up divorced. Statistically speaking, this could have been a reality for me, but thank God, Cathe and I recently celebrated 52 years of marriage.

God wants to bless our marriages. After all, it was God who designed it. He originated it, uniquely established it, and gave it as a blessing to humanity. Because of this, one of Satan's greatest goals in our culture and in this time in which we live is to destroy as many marriages as he possibly can. And he doesn't much care whether those couples are Christians or not.

If he or his demons can find a crack or a crevice in a marriage, and somehow gain a foothold, they'll try to exploit it to the max. As Paul told the church in Ephesus, "If you are angry, don't sin by nursing your grudge. Don't let the sun go down with you still angry—get over it quickly; for when you are angry, you give a mighty foothold to the devil" (Ephesians 4:26–27 TLB).

The evil one is looking for handholds, footholds, toeholds, any kind of holds in your marriage. He has set his sights on the family, and nothing would delight him more than to see it destroyed—especially Christian families. That is why we want to do everything we can to draw a line around our homes and say, "This belongs to the Lord. We will do this God's way, building our marriage on God's principles."

Not Just Finding, but "Being"

There's no use denying it: We live in a culture that is openly hostile to the institutions of marriage and family. Activists do everything in their power to undermine and redefine what marriage and family really are. Using the tools of humor and cynicism, novelists, songwriters, and TV/movie writers deliberately mock and ridicule traditional roles, values, and families.

The culture's alternative is to "seek your own happiness and pleasure, no matter what the cost." (Aren't you hearing this kind of messaging everywhere you turn?) We are essentially told to believe, "Everything revolves around me. I am the only one who ultimately matters."

Concepts like sacrifice, selflessness, and keeping one's commitments are rarely heard of today, and we carry the same, selfish, "me-first" mentality into our marriages. We say to ourselves, "I will marry you so you can make me a happy person. As long as you fulfill me and meet my needs, I will stay with you, that is, unless someone better or more interesting comes along."

We might not come right out and say that, but judging by the way many people act and behave today, it is a reality. Please understand what I'm saying here. I'm not suggesting you can't be happy and fulfilled in a marriage. I'm saying that if you enter into marriage with the sole expectation of your spouse meeting *your* needs, without any real concern about you meeting *theirs*, you will be disappointed.

Marriage depends on two things: finding the right person and *being* the right person. We like to skip the second half of this equation, don't we?

The right motive is wanting to marry someone so you can make *them* happy, meet *their* needs, and bring *them* fulfillment. That should be the motive. Yet self-obsession is rampant in our society today. In fact, the Bible tells us it will be paramount in the last days, a time in which I believe we are now living.

According to 2 Timothy 3:1–4, "In the last days perilous times will come: For men will be lovers of themselves, lovers of money, boasters, proud, blasphemers, disobedient to parents, unthankful, unholy, unloving, unforgiving, slanderers, without self-control, brutal, despisers of good, traitors, headstrong, haughty, lovers of pleasure rather than lovers of God" (NKJV).

Maybe you're thinking, "Wait a second. I thought we needed to love ourselves. I've always heard that the biggest problem in our culture was a lack of self-love. I thought that all of the problems of our culture could be traced to low self-esteem and poor self-image."

Or so we are led to believe.

But the Bible tells us that one of the signs of the last days is that people will love themselves more than they love God. And it is because of our self-love—our fixation and obsession with self—that we find ourselves facing so many problems and heartaches in today's culture.

In our entertainment-saturated society, we are living in an altered state of reality. We live with illusions of what life should be—the fantasy of the perfect romantic and sexual relationship, the perfect spouse, and the perfect lifestyle. Yet what we're chasing after doesn't even exist. And when life doesn't measure up to what we think it should, we simply say, "I'll go and look for it somewhere else." This often includes bailing out on a marriage.

Not Being Consumers but "Communers"

As Christians, we must abandon this unbiblical and destructive type of thinking. God has called us, as His children, to a different standard. He has called us to a higher level of living, a new way of thinking and behaving.

I think the reason we have seen the social fabric of our society begin to break down, and the overall morality of America decline, is because to many, the church has become a commodity. We have put our pleasure and our enjoyment ahead of God's glory, and our consumerist mentality has actually broken the first commandment, which is to "have no other gods before Me" (Exodus 20:3 NKJV).

In nearly every aspect of life, we have put ourselves first. At one time, church was the place to worship and glorify God. Now what has it become? All about us.

Who's leading worship today?

Who's preaching today?

What's the weather like?

Is there a game on?

We're willing to show up if all the stars perfectly align, and only then will we show up 15 minutes late and leave 10 minutes early. (Ouch)

If we train up consumers instead of communers, we will end up with customers instead of disciples.

Doesn't this apply to marriage as well? If you view your role with a consumerist mentality, you aren't going to be a devoted spouse. Instead, you'll be a customer. In effect, your spouse becomes a product, something you enjoy as long as they hold up to your standards. Once they no longer meet your needs, you want to exchange them for a newer, better model. But let's be clear: We do not want to be customers. We want to be lifelong companions living in communion with God and each other.

Here are some great reminders from Scripture:

Ephesians 4:1–2 tells us, "Walk worthy of the calling with which you were called, with all lowliness and gentleness, with longsuffering, bearing with one another in love" (NKJV).

Second Corinthians 6:17 says, "Come out from among them and be separate" (NKJV).

Romans 12:2 reads, "Don't let the world around you squeeze you into its own mould, but let God re-mould your minds from within, so that you may prove in practice that the plan of God for you is good, meets all his demands and moves towards the goal of true maturity" (PHI).

With God's help, we must reject selfishness, and in its place, find a new, selfless, God-honoring life in which we put God's Word above our own desires. If we want our marriages to be strong, we must value obedience to God and the needs of our spouse on a distinctly higher scale than our own wants and wishes.

While our culture tells us that self-esteem ought to be our brightest and most important guiding star, the Bible tells us otherwise: "Let nothing be done through selfish ambition or conceit, but in lowliness of mind let each esteem others better than himself. Let each of you look out not only for his own interests, but also for the interests of others" (Philippians 2:3–4 NKJV).

If every married couple did this alone, our homes would be transformed overnight. If you put the needs of your wife or husband above your own, and thought of their happiness and their fulfillment over yours, it would radically change your relationship. And you know what?

All that happiness would flow right back to you.

Not Pointing Blame, but Accepting Responsibility

This, of course, not only flies in the face of cultural norms and expectations, but it also moves cross-current to our basic human nature. It all goes back to a very dark day in that paradise called Eden:

> Now the serpent was more cunning than any beast of the field which the LORD God had made. And he said to the woman, "Has God indeed said, 'You shall not eat of every tree of the garden'?" And the woman said to the serpent, "We may eat the fruit of the trees of the garden; but of the fruit of the tree which is in the midst of the garden, God has said, 'You shall not eat it, nor shall you touch it, lest you die.'" Then the serpent said to the woman, "You will not surely die. For God knows that in the day you eat of it your eyes will be opened, and you will be like God, knowing good and evil." So when the woman saw that the tree was good for food, that it was pleasant to the eyes, and a tree desirable to make one wise, she took of its fruit and ate. She also gave to her husband with her, and he ate. Then the eyes of both of them were opened. (Genesis 3:1–7 NKJV)

Eve was at the wrong place, at the wrong time, listening to the wrong voice, which led her to do the wrong thing. Adam soon joined her, and when confronted by God for an explanation of his disobedience, he gave the first excuse recorded in human history. Adam said, "The woman whom You gave to be with me, she gave me of the tree, and I ate" (verse 12).

What a lame, cowardly thing to say.

You and I weren't there to hear the inflections of his voice, so we don't know how he spoke these words. (With a whine, maybe?) It could have come down to which word he emphasized in that sentence. For instance, if Adam said, "It's the *woman* You gave me," he was placing the blame on Eve, not himself. Conversely, if he said, "It's the woman *You* gave me," he would have been blaming God. Either way, it was a pitiful excuse. Adam was fully responsible for his own actions. Eve didn't fare much better as she tried to blame it all on Satan, as if she'd had nothing to do with it. "The serpent deceived me, and I ate" (verse 13).

Loosely paraphrased: "It's not my fault; the devil made me do it."

When you engage in sin, it's easy to point blame without taking responsibility. And isn't this what Jesus warned against in Matthew 7:3–5, about picking the splinter out of your brother's eye without taking the log out of your own? Adam and Eve had no excuse. Both of them crossed the line, knowing only too well that it was the wrong thing to do. As a result of that sin, a curse came upon humanity, and we feel its repercussions to this very day. As a result of this curse, a number of very dark things entered into the human race, starting with death, the darkest of all.

A Terrible New Reality

Up to this point, Adam and Eve would not have faced death, disease, or the aging process. But because of their sin, the curse of sickness, a limited lifespan, and the ultimate termination of life on earth began. Remember, God said, "But of the tree of the knowledge of good and evil you shall not eat, for in the day that you eat of it you shall surely die" (Genesis 2:17 NKJV). When they ate of it, they experienced the promised consequence, and the long shadow of death fell over the human race.

Another part of this curse was multiplied pain at childbirth: "To the woman He said: 'I will greatly multiply your sorrow and your conception; in pain you shall bring forth children'" (Genesis 3:16 NKJV). The wonderful joy of giving birth to a child would now be impacted and overshadowed by intense physical pain.

Prior to the birth of our two boys, I went through the natural childbirth classes with Cathe. To alleviate the pain of contractions, she practiced her breathing techniques; I was her "coach." She did a great job bringing our sons into this world. But she also went through all of the pain. Let me just say that I'm thankful this part of the curse didn't fall on men! I would never have held up as well as she did.

We men, however, also have our part of the curse to bear, which is strenuous work. Prior to his fall into sin, Adam's job was primarily to enjoy the glory and splendor of what God had made. But now he would have to labor hard and long to somehow scratch a living out of the earth.

In Genesis 3, God said to Adam, "Cursed is the ground for your sake; in toil you shall eat of it all the days of your life. Both thorns and thistles it shall bring forth for you, and you shall eat the herb of the field. In the sweat of your face you shall eat bread till you return to the ground, for out of it you were taken; for dust you are, and to dust you shall return" (verses 17–19 NKJV).

A Battle of the Sexes

Another aspect of the curse that fell on humanity still affects our marriages to this day: strife and selfishness. After Eve sinned in the Garden of Eden, which was a result of her disobedience to God and her failure to consult with Adam about the serpent's temptation, the Lord had something very important to say to her.

He said: "Your desire shall be for your husband, and he shall rule over you" (verse 16 NKJV).

When we read these words, it's important to keep in mind that this statement was part of the curse. Looking at the words in the original language will help us understand a dynamic that causes tension between men and women to this very day and explains the reason for a "battle of the sexes."

The word God used for *desire* is the same one also used in Genesis 4:7 (the identical Hebrew term) and comes from a root word that means "to compel, to impel, to urge, or to seek control over."

Using the same word in Genesis 4:7, the Lord warned Cain, "Sin lies at the door. And its desire is for you, but you should rule over it" (NKJV).

God was essentially saying, "Cain, sin wants to control you, but you must control sin."

In light of this close contextual meaning of the word *desire*, the curse on Eve was that woman's desire would be to henceforth usurp the place of her husband's headship. In other words, she would want to rule her husband, but he would rule over her.

If you are a man reading these words, you may be thinking, "Preach it, Greg. This is good stuff! I like this." But hold on a minute. This is a double-edged sword because the word used in this verse for *rule* is a word that means "to subdue, to put under your feet."

This is part of the curse, too, and it wasn't something God was advocating. Rather, it was something that God was *acknowledging* as a result of sin. In other words, it was speaking of a new kind of authoritarianism that was not in God's original plan for man's headship. The distortion of woman's proper submissiveness and man's proper authority came as a direct result of Adam and Eve's sin and the curse that followed.

This is where male chauvinism and women's liberation have their origins. Woman has a sinful inclination to usurp the authority of her husband, and man has a sinful inclination to put his wife under his feet. Both are equally wrong before God.

Standing Equally, Functioning Differently

Some people today assert that the Bible is a sexist book. Yet anyone who makes a statement like that demonstrates an obvious ignorance of Scripture and biblical culture. We have to examine what the Bible is really saying and dispel this ridiculous thinking.

If anything, the Bible and its message *liberated* women. The apostle Paul, who has been wrongly labeled a chauvinist by some, said, "Husbands, love your wives, just as Christ also loved the church and gave Himself for her" (Ephesians 5:25 NKJV).

Many of us have heard these words before, perhaps many times. Still, this was *revolutionary* stuff for the time in which Paul was living. Telling a husband to love his wife as Christ loved the church, to give himself for her, was a radically different message from what husbands had heard up to that point.

In Roman culture, women were treated as possessions rather than partners in life. Even in the Jewish culture of the day, a man might divorce his wife for practically any reason, though he had to warp and twist Scripture to do it. So, let's not take today's secular thinking and try to attach it to Scripture. The Bible gives us the truth about how we are to live and function.

Men and women are equal before God, but we are different. Our roles are different as well. When we fail to see that, we make a big mistake. God has wired men and women in different ways, and He uses us in different ways. Instead of being upset about it, we should celebrate it and rejoice in it because it all works out in His plan and His balance.

Looking in the Mirror

The problem with most marriages today is not money, careers, sex, children, in-laws, or any of those typical reasons people give. No, it really boils down to one word: *Self.*

We love to blame this thing or that thing for our marital difficulties, but the real problem looks back at us in the mirror.

James asks, "What is causing the quarrels and fights among you? Isn't it because there is a whole army of evil desires at war within you?" (James 4:1 TLB).

We could complain and vent for hours about one issue or another in our marriage, but here's the hard truth: We bring these problems into our marriages because of our sinful bent and our natural orientation toward pleasing ourselves.

Of course, no one would ever actually say it that way. Instead, we hear the same inane, tired phrases so devoid of real content and so terribly destructive.

"I'm no longer happy in my marriage."

"I need some time for me."

"I need my own space."

"My wife/husband is no longer meeting my needs."

"I'm going to go find myself."

It's this ridiculous, selfish orientation that destroys so many marriages, homes, and families with reverberations that roll on for generations. While it's true that selfishness is part of human nature, it is not true that we're beyond the hope of changing.

The Bible tells us, "If anyone is in Christ, he is a new creation; old things have passed away; behold, all things have become new" (2 Corinthians 5:17 NKJV).

God is telling us that we have a new nature, and that we are to live by new standards. But here's the best part: He has given us new power to accomplish those very things.

Prayer: Lord, thank You for Your perfect design. Although we are imperfect people, we have Your Spirit to help us walk in obedience to You. In every relationship, every season, and every trial, You equip us with everything we need. Thank You, Lord. Help us remain steadfast in our marriages and families, standing strong against the enemy's lies. Strengthen us to do whatever it takes to live in unity with You and each other. We need You, Lord. Every step of the way, we need You. In Jesus' name, amen.

QUESTIONS for Discussion

1. Greg shared that, statistically speaking, divorce could have become his reality, but instead, he and Cathe have been married for over 50 years. How are you and your spouse defying the odds? What principles do you have in place to safeguard against the rising tide of divorce in today's culture?

2. Reflect on Ephesians 4:26–27 for a moment: "If you are angry, don't sin by nursing your grudge. Don't let the sun go down with you still angry—get over it quickly; for when you are angry, you give a mighty foothold to the devil" (TLB). In addition to unresolved anger, what are some other footholds that Satan might try to exploit to damage the closeness between a husband and wife?

3. The right motive for marriage is to make your spouse happy, meet *their* needs, and bring *them* fulfillment. How does this advice go against the grain of what our culture advocates? How can we keep from being influenced by the culture's unending "me-first" emphasis?

4. This chapter says, "If you view your [marital] role with a consumerist

mentality, you aren't going to be a devoted spouse. Instead, you'll be a customer. In effect, your spouse becomes a product, something you enjoy as long as they hold up to your standards. Once they no longer meet your needs, you want to exchange them for a newer, better model." How could a consumerist mentality cause insecurity and lack of devotion in marriage? And how does Philippians 2:3–4 solve this issue?

5. After God confronted Adam with his disobedience and sin, Adam said, "The woman whom You gave to be with me, she gave me of the tree, and I ate" (Genesis 3:12 NKJV). Greg calls this the world's first lame excuse. And Eve essentially said, "The devil made me do it." In what ways do we continue this trend of blaming "someone else" for our marriage difficulties, rather than facing up to hard truths about ourselves?

6. We read, "When you engage in sin, it's easy to point blame without taking responsibility." How does this relate to Matthew 7:3–5, about picking the splinter out of your brother's eye without taking the log out of your own?

7. The biblical definition for *desire* is "to compel, to impel, to urge, or to seek control over." We also see the meaning of the word *rule* as "to subdue, or put under your feet." How does this "curse" still affect marriages today? In what way has it contributed to feminism and chauvinism?

8. It is explained that "God has wired men and women in different ways, and He uses us in different ways. Instead of being upset about it, we should celebrate it and rejoice in it, because it all works out in His plan and His balance." Give some real-life examples of when this God-ordained balance has worked out well. What happens when we refuse to acknowledge that men and women are equal but different?

9. The chapter says, "We could complain and vent for hours about one issue or another in our marriage, but here's the hard truth: We bring these problems into our marriages because of our sinful bent and

our natural orientation toward pleasing ourselves." To what extent do you agree or disagree with this statement? If you agree that this is true, what can you and your spouse do about it? How can "looking in the mirror" resolve or put into perspective most marital issues?

10. The Bible tells us, "If anyone is in Christ, he is a new creation; old things have passed away; behold, all things have become new" (2 Corinthians 5:17 NKJV). How does this verse compel us to live according to new, higher standards? Who empowers us to be able to do this?

Preparing Your Heart First

"Lord, you know the hopes of humble people. Surely you will hear their cries and comfort their hearts by helping them." —Psalm 10:17 (TLB)

You can try to build a marriage on wealth and success, or physical appearance and mutual attraction, saying, "Oh, he's just so handsome, and she's just so beautiful; we go together like Ken and Barbie." Whatever. And what about sexual chemistry? Or your common love for a TV show, sports team, kittens, veganism . . . the list goes on. There are countless things you could build your marriage upon, but the reality is, when the storms of life come and you get that unwanted phone call, there's only one thing that will sustain you: the hope that comes from being in a relationship with Jesus Christ. He is the Rock on which to build lasting relationships.

In Matthew 7:24–27, Jesus said:

> Anyone who listens to my teaching and follows it is wise, like a person who builds a house on solid rock. Though the rain comes in torrents and the floodwaters rise, and the winds beat against that house, it won't collapse because it is built on bedrock. But anyone who hears my teaching and doesn't obey it is foolish, like a person who builds a house on sand. When the rains and floods come and the winds beat against that house, it will collapse with a mighty crash. (NLT)

Preparing your heart for marriage includes building on a solid foundation. So, when the rain does come, and the waters do rise, and the floodwaters do rush in, and the winds do blow, your house, your spiritual life, and your marriage will not collapse. And listen, it's not just the storms of life that you will encounter as a couple, including storms of suffering, storms of sickness, storms of job loss, etc. No, it's also the smaller storms of frustration, arguments, disagreements, and not getting along.

How do you reconcile if you don't have your foundation built on Jesus Christ?

We've all seen celebrity marriages over the years that last anywhere from a few years to a few days. You don't read about many that last more than a decade, and what are they built on? Well, often they're built on fame and fortune, or appearance and sexuality. Whatever it is, it isn't stable. It does not weather the storms of life. They are not built on a spiritual foundation rooted in Christ.

If a couple has faith in Jesus, they have a deeper commitment to the Lord than to each other. We always want to be obedient to Jesus and His call for our lives.

So, when you are choosing that girl or guy you're wanting to date, you want to make sure you aim for someone who has the faith you want to have. When you're looking for Mr. or Miss Right, look for somebody who is spiritually stronger than you are. Ask the Lord to make the decision on your behalf, praying, "Lord, I don't know who to look for; I don't know where to go; I don't know who the right person is. Would you choose for me, Lord?"

Now, some of you might actually be terrified to ask God to choose for you. You're thinking, "He's gonna choose somebody I'm not attracted to." But listen, the guy or girl you want to date might be hot, but so is Hell, okay? (Just kidding.) God is not going to make you date somebody ugly, alright? He's not going to make you marry somebody that you are not attracted to. He's going to bring you exactly the right person, and the best thing that you could do is ask God to choose for you.

Choosing God's Way

God's way is the only way I want for something as precious and valuable as my marriage. By saying that, I'm also saying that I *don't* want marriage the world's way. The world—and by that, I mean our culture—is largely hostile toward the family and everything it stands for. I have never known another time when the family has been under attack as it is today from those who not only want to undermine it, but to even redefine it.

The good news is this: We don't have to rely on our culture's constantly morphing definition of marriage and family. No matter how dominant and insistent that voice might become, we don't have to look for secular advice on how to succeed in marriage and life. We have something *far* better.

We have the eternal, unchanging, utterly reliable Word of God.

We have the ultimate Guidebook to tell us how to have a happy and successful marriage.

The Bible warns us that the enemy's goal has always been to steal, kill, and destroy, but Jesus came to give us life, and life more abundantly (see John 10:10). The devil would love nothing more than to steal the truth from us, kill our desire to follow God's Word, and twist what it means to have a happy marriage.

But as a truth-teller, I take every chance I can get to proclaim God's Word. And that's what we need. More truth-tellers.

Dating with Marriage in Mind

Some people believe dating is an opportunity to "sow your wild oats." I hate that statement. People might as well say, "Go get a venereal disease," or "Go get pregnant by some random person." This is horrible.

The cultural message is: "You have to test drive the car to make sure it's a good fit for you. Have sex, move in together, focus on what you want." But please hear me on this. God has a plan. He has an outline for you. Dating isn't "sowing our wild oats," but preparing our hearts for marriage.

Jonathan's Story: When Brittni and I were in premarital counseling, and the pastor asked, "Have you guys ever gotten in a fight?"

I was like, "No, never. I mean, we've argued and stuff, but we've never really gotten into a real fight." He said, "Okay. Well, you probably will. It might even happen on your honeymoon, so just be prepared for that. And by the way, here's how to fight fair."

He wasn't trying to scare us, but *prepare* us. And honestly, I thought we were prepared. But I will tell you right now, there's a huge difference between knowing what you're supposed to do and *doing* what you're supposed to do. You can read all the books and learn how to fight fair, but ultimately, you're dealing with one very large variable: people.

We're human beings, right? We have emotions, we have wills, and we have opinions of what we think is best. We are imperfect people who get married to someone who is also imperfect. Dating with marriage in mind means you go into it with your eyes wide open. In the words of Benjamin Franklin, "Keep your eyes wide open before marriage, and half-shut afterwards."

Hoping to Fix Them? (Ain't Gonna Happen)

To be totally honest with you, marriage doesn't fix who you are. It *shows* you who you are. I'm telling you, marriage will show you faster than anything all of your ugly flaws. If you think about it, you're bringing a person—another sinful, flawed person—into close proximity, living with you under the same roof. So, guess what? You're seeing all their flaws too.

If you're hoping to fix someone after you get married, I hate to break it to you, but it ain't gonna happen. If you want a great marriage, you're going to have to work hard at it. God will give you the grace and strength as you seek Him and recognize that you are both married to sinners. And somehow, by the grace of God, in the middle of all your flaws, the Holy Spirit can transform you.

So, if you pick a guy or girl thinking, "I'm going to marry them and fix them," don't marry them. Because here's reality, they may end up worse than they are now. Chances are, they're going to become a more exaggerated version of the person you now see. So, if you're not okay with that, if you can't live with that, then maybe you shouldn't pursue that person.

Following Your Impulses Is a Bad Idea

While you are dating, make it your goal to glorify God. Follow His plan and His will, rather than your desires and impulses. Seek to edify each other by building each other up, praying for each other, reading Scripture together, and calling each other to spiritual depth. These are ways to prepare your heart and your relationship as you are dating.

The cultural goal is to "fall in love with each other," and that sounds great, right? But falling in love comes naturally over time. What you want to do is set the foundation so that you'll have a successful marriage. This includes having a successful courting period, a dating season that aligns with God's design, not the culture.

> Jonathan's Perspective: Believe it or not, I never dated my wife, Brittni. I never asked her out on a date, even though I thought she was cute the first time I saw her. No. She showed up at a Bible study, and we chatted afterwards. Then, I aggressively stalked her on social media. (Just kidding!)
>
> Over time, we got to know each other. I saw how she interacted with people. She saw how I interacted with people.
>
> And gradually, the group got smaller and smaller and smaller, until we realized, "Hey, we both like each other." That's when we started our courtship, our relationship. There was never a moment where it was like, "Will you be my wedded girlfriend?"
>
> When you're ready to date, become friends with the person first, and see what God is doing in their life. See if they are a good match for you.
>
> Brittni and I prayed for each other. We prayed *with* each other. We had both made the decision to pursue a relationship with God first, and tell others about what God was doing in our lives. It was an intentional friendship that had marriage as the goal.
>
> So, I found a wife the one time in my young adult life that I was not trying to find a girlfriend. I was simply pursuing God. Everything that I had looked for in this world had let me down. All the decisions that I had made screwed things up. And you

know what? My relationship with the Lord was the one thing that had not let me down.

And so, as I pursued God first, putting Him as number one, He brought me the thing that I had been looking for all along: a relationship with this girl. And now we've been married for over 15 years. I'm so thankful He did that. And I'm thankful, too, that He didn't bring her to me a year or two earlier. God's timing is perfect. So, the best thing you can do for your Christian dating is to put God first. Then, as you grow together, keeping Jesus at the center of your relationship, you want to hear people say, "Wow, you guys aren't having sex before you get married? You're not living together before you get married?"

You can confidently respond with, "No, we're not going to do those things. We're going through premarital counseling, and we're learning about what marriage truly is. We're learning why God has put us together, and how to prepare our hearts for conflict resolution. Instead of running away when conflicts arise, we are actually committed to a deeper relationship because of what God has called us to."

If I told you everything I knew about the ocean and surfing, and promised to take you out tomorrow, you'd be taking diligent notes because you'd want to be prepared. But as soon as you got caught in the impact zone, with a wave breaking right in front of you, all that knowledge would go right out of your head. You'd forget everything I taught you and follow your instincts. You'd panic and want to go up when you should go down. You'd want to run away when you should run toward the waves.

Following your impulses instead of God's plan will always lead you in the wrong direction. So, what does the Bible have to say about God's plan?

What the Bible Says
The Word of God doesn't just give us beautiful language or lofty ideals. No, the Bible is *alive* with truth—truth that works and changes and transforms lives. It also changes marriages. I've seen it happen more times than I can count.

But sometimes, people don't like or appreciate what the Bible teaches about the role of the husband and the wife. In fact, it runs directly counter to strong opinions in today's culture. Nevertheless, it is the Word of God; it is true, and remains steadfast no matter how the culture shifts and changes all around it.

Second Timothy 2:19 says, "Nevertheless, God's solid foundation stands firm, sealed with this inscription: 'The Lord knows those who are his,' and, 'Everyone who confesses the name of the Lord must turn away from wickedness'" (NIV).

God's Word stands firm to this very day.

Sometimes, when people come to me for marriage counseling, it means they've tried everything else, and this is the last resort. By the time they think of "talking to the pastor," their relationship may be hanging by a thread. When I sit down with a couple for our initial counseling session, the first question I ask is if they're both Christians. They usually say yes. Then I ask them if they both believe the Bible is the Word of God. Again, they usually reply in the affirmative.

But *then* I ask them, "Are you willing to do what the Bible says, even if you find it difficult?" That's when the hesitation begins. They shoot each other glances and realize that if they say yes, they'll be stepping into my trap. Even so, it's an all-important question for that couple—or any couple. Why?

Because I have never found a couple contemplating divorce who were truly doing what the Word of God says they should do in their marriage.

What's more, I don't think I ever will. If a husband and wife are willing in their hearts to roll up their sleeves and actually do what God says, they won't have to worry about divorce court in their future. But if they reject, water down, or compromise the Bible's clear principles, they will find trouble up ahead.

Some of the best marriage counsel in the Bible can be found in the fifth chapter of Paul's letter to the church at Ephesus, and we will explore those verses in the next chapter. But before the apostle starts giving specific advice for wives and husbands, he does a little vision-casting. He shows us how to prepare our lives in order to become the best marriage partner we can be.

Walking in Light of Ephesians 5

When you walk into a really nice restaurant or a beautiful home, you're immediately struck by the view. Perhaps the first thing you see as you enter through the front door, are large windows with a panoramic view of the ocean, the mountains, the city lights, or some other striking scene. It's so inviting. It's the kind of room where you want to linger.

So it is when you walk through the "doorway" of Ephesians 5. The view of marriage from this chapter elevates the relationship of husband and wife to amazing new heights. It's living truth, strong truth, and beautiful truth.

Before he addresses the specifics of marriage, though, the apostle Paul gets down to the nitty-gritty in this section of his letter, dealing with issues and temptations we face even as Christians. He begins by telling them,

> Therefore be imitators of God as dear children. And walk in love, as Christ also has loved us and given Himself for us, an offering and a sacrifice to God for a sweet-smelling aroma.

> But fornication and all uncleanness or covetousness, let it not even be named among you, as is fitting for saints; neither filthiness, nor foolish talking, nor coarse jesting, which are not fitting, but rather giving of thanks. For this you know, that no fornicator, unclean person, nor covetous man, who is an idolater, has any inheritance in the kingdom of Christ and God. Let no one deceive you with empty words, for because of these things the wrath of God comes upon the sons of disobedience. Therefore do not be partakers with them.

> For you were once darkness, but now you are light in the Lord. Walk as children of light (for the fruit of the Spirit is in all goodness, righteousness, and truth), finding out what is acceptable to the Lord. And have no fellowship with the unfruitful

works of darkness, but rather expose them. For it is shameful even to speak of those things which are done by them in secret. (Ephesians 5:1–12 NKJV)

"Dear children." That's a nice phrase, isn't it? The fact is you aren't simply a child of God; you are a dear—beloved—child of God. Do you realize how much God loves you? Are you aware of the depth of His affection toward you?

When the Lord Jesus was baptized by John, the Father spoke from Heaven and said, "You are My beloved Son, in whom I am well pleased" (Mark 1:11 NKJV).

We know that God the Father was very pleased with His Son. God loved and loves His Son, the Lord Jesus Christ. "That's great," you say. "But that's Jesus. That's not me." But listen to these amazing words that Jesus uttered in His prayer in the Gospel of John. He said: "I have given them the glory that you gave me, that they may be one as we are one—I in them and you in me—so that they may be brought to complete unity" (John 17:22–23 NIV).

What? Could that really be true?

Did Jesus really say that the Father loves us as much as He loves Jesus? If the Lord Himself hadn't said it, I wouldn't even dare to suggest such a thing. Yet this is exactly what the Bible teaches. You are a dear and deeply loved child of God.

So . . . let's start *living* that way.

Many times, you and I don't behave like dearly loved, highly valued children of the living God. But that's precisely what we are. We have been adopted into His family with full rights and privileges. The Bible says that when we become believers in Jesus, we are "accepted in the Beloved" (Ephesians 1:6 NKJV). And that simply means that now God sees you in His Son, Jesus Christ. He doesn't see you for what you were; He sees you for what you are—and what He will make you into!

How should the knowledge that we are accepted in this way by God—that we are His dear children—affect us in the way we live in this world? It should affect us in several ways.

1. It should help me to avoid immorality

Ephesians 5:3 says: "But fornication and all uncleanness or covetousness, let it not even be named among you, as is fitting for saints" (NKJV).

Now why would Paul bring up such unsavory topics like these? It helps to understand the situation these believers lived in at that time. Ephesus was the capital of the Roman province of Asia, a busy and affluent commercial port. But it was also cult headquarters for the goddess Diana.

Immorality was rampant throughout the city. Thousands of prostitutes working for the temple would comb the streets of the city, looking for potential recruits. They would lure men into the temple to engage in sexual rites as they offered worship to this false deity. So, these Ephesian believers were godly people living in a godless place. Paul told them, in effect, "I want to just spell it out for you guys. As followers of Jesus, you can't live a compromised lifestyle. No more of this!"

Is this an appropriate word for today's culture? You'd better believe it. We, too, are sex-obsessed and bombarded on all sides with invitations to fornication and immorality.

What is *fornication*, anyway? It is sex outside of marriage, and there is never any justification, rationale, or "special allowance" for that. It is *always* a sin before God.

But Paul doesn't just mention that. He also mentions "uncleanness" and "covetousness," saying that we shouldn't allow even a *hint* of these things in our lives. Not a hint! That's very important. This, I believe, speaks to our electronic culture. We may not (technically) be engaging in extramarital sex, doing the twisted things that wicked people do, but we can *watch* them do these things on our TVs, laptops, and phones.

In the sick, voyeuristic world we live in today, we can follow the latest antics of godless actors and entertainers who post their activities on You-Tube or X (Twitter). I have never seen so much interest in the lifestyles of these so-called celebrities like we see today.

And what does Paul say about it? He says you are an imitator of God, and a treasured child of God. Not only should you not do those things, but there shouldn't even be a hint of this stuff in your life. Then he takes it a step further.

2. *It should motivate me to avoid obscene talk*

Look at Ephesians 5, verse 4: "Neither filthiness, nor foolish talking, nor coarse jesting, which are not fitting, but rather giving of thanks" (NKJV).

"Filthiness" has to do with general obscenity—talk that is disgraceful and degrading. Paul also mentions coarse jesting, which covers the double entendre and sexual innuendo.

Some people can turn anything into a weird joke. They begin to see everything through the lens of sexual obsession, and distort innocent remarks into off-color "humor." In other words, their minds and hearts are so full of their obsessions that it colors their life and speech.

Paul essentially says, "No! it should not be that way among God's children."

And it most certainly shouldn't be that way among pastors, who are specifically called to be examples to the flock (see 1 Peter 5:3). Strange as it may seem, there's a popular trend in some churches today for pastors to use obscene language in the pulpit. Some think that sort of thing is "daring" or "relevant" or "authentic."

No, it's just plain wrong.

If that's what I have to do as a pastor to stay relevant, then I will be irrelevant. The fact is you can be authentic without crossing the line of decency. You can be down-to-earth without being "earthy." Make sense?

There is also a trend in some churches today to use an emphasis on sex to attract crowds. They will have a series on the book of Song of Solomon, which is fine because it's a book in the Bible and inspired by God. But they will teach it as though it was some kind of explicit sex manual, instead of presenting it with respect, delicacy, and honor. In this way, these teachers play to the epicurean interests of a twisted culture. And all of this is done in the name of reenvisioning or reimagining church.

We don't need to do that. We don't need to reenvision or reimagine church. We don't need to reenvision or reimagine the meaning of Scripture. We need to rediscover and reveal God's truth the way He intended it.

3. It should motivate me to avoid coveting

Moving to verse 5, Paul says: "For this you know, that no fornicator, unclean person, nor covetous man, who is an idolater, has any inheritance in the kingdom of Christ and God" (NKJV).

What is coveting? You could actually translate the word *covet* to "pant after." Picture a thirsty animal with its tongue hanging out. That's the concept here, and it isn't very attractive. To covet is to eagerly desire or set your heart on something (or someone) that belongs to another. It might be your neighbor's wife or husband, or it might be something they own that you don't.

Remember the story of David and Bathsheba? David saw a beautiful woman from his palace balcony, and he coveted her. She was someone else's wife, but he didn't care. King David didn't resist his impulse, and he sent someone to go get her. And we all know how that turned out.

Paul teaches us that covetousness doesn't belong in one of God's sons or daughters.

4. It should encourage me to walk in a new way

In Ephesians 5: 8–10 we read: "For you were once darkness, but now you are light in the Lord. Walk as children of light (for the fruit of the Spirit is in all goodness, righteousness, and truth), finding out what is acceptable to the Lord" (NKJV).

Paul uses three words to describe how we are to walk as believers: in *goodness*, in *righteousness*, and in *truth*.

How should we walk?

In *goodness*. A better translation of the word would be "generosity." Godly people should be generous people, not stingy.

How should we walk?

In *righteousness*. In this context, this speaks of integrity in our dealings with others. Christians should be godly and aboveboard in all their business dealings. You can't shrug and say, "Well, business is business." That may very well be the same as saying, "Hey, I'll do whatever it takes to get ahead in my particular line of work." It's good to excel in our jobs or professions, and to succeed to the best of our abilities. But we also need to do our work with honesty and integrity.

How should we walk?

In *truth*. This means an absence of falsehood and deception. Godly people should be honest people. But that's not all. Godly people have yet another obligation.

5. *It should embolden me to confront sin*

Ephesians 5:11 says, "Have no fellowship with the unfruitful works of darkness, but rather expose them" (NKJV). This gets tricky now, because the watchwords of our day are tolerance, acceptance, and understanding. According to our contemporary culture, there is no higher value than tolerance.

Sometimes in the course of teaching the Bible, I'll highlight a particular teaching that's making the rounds in our country, and I will say, "According to the Bible, this teaching is wrong."

Occasionally someone will tell me, "Pastor, what you said wasn't loving."

But it is loving. As a shepherd, I'm seeking to protect God's people from a teaching or direction that could harm them. How is that not loving? It would be like seeing a wolf sneak through a hole in the fence while your toddler plays in the backyard, and you drive that wolf away with a stick.

Is that "loving"?

Well, maybe not for the wolf. But it is for the child! For the sake of a little one, I would repel that predator with harsh measures, and do so without a pang of conscience. In the same way, we have to confront sin when we see it.

But don't expect to win any popularity contests for doing that. If you speak out for what is true, you will quickly be branded as intolerant, bigoted, puritanical, and narrow. Be that as it may, the Bible tells us, "Have no fellowship with the unfruitful works of darkness, but rather expose them" (Ephesians 5:11 NKJV). To "expose" carries the idea of reproof, correction, punishment, or discipline. It is to confront sin. So, if you have a friend who claims to be a follower of Jesus, and you see him or her making serious moral compromises, you need to confront that friend.

Just make sure you do so with love and wisdom.

We all know people who feel it's their job to be professional confronters, and are just a little too quick on the draw to condemn everything. At the same time, however, there are many more people who are so reticent and passive that they never face up to evil at all, and refuse to deal with anything.

Scripture gives us a great model in the person of Nathan the prophet. As mentioned above, King David had fallen into sin, committing adultery with Bathsheba. He then arranged for her husband's death in battle. He had not repented of those sins, and he lived like that for a full year. Nathan bided his time, waiting for the right moment to approach the king. Finally, he told David a story about a stolen lamb, and the king took the bait, proclaiming that the heartless, selfish individual who stole that little lamb deserved to die. Nathan looked David right in the eyes and boldly said, "You are the man!" (2 Samuel 12:7 NIV).

Nathan knew very well the king could have had his head for that confrontation. But the godly prophet must have said in his heart, "So be it. I can't allow my friend to go on living a lie, and in rebellion against God." So, he spoke up, in spite of the risk.

When we confront someone, we must go in humility and love, speaking the truth to those who need to hear it. That's what God's Word is telling us.

Turn on the Light

Finally, in Ephesians 5:13–16, Paul says, "But all things that are exposed are made manifest by the light, for whatever makes manifest is light. Therefore He says: 'Awake, you who sleep, arise from the dead, and Christ will give you light.' See then that you walk circumspectly, not as fools but as wise, redeeming the time, because the days are evil" (NKJV).

Reiterating verse 13, we read, "But all things that are exposed are made manifest by the light, for whatever makes manifest is light."

Have you ever misplaced anything in the dark? How do you find it again unless you turn on the light? Sometimes, when I'm getting ready in the morning, I'll dress in the dark so I don't disturb my wife. But then, when I get out into the light, I see what I have on and realize, "Oh . . . this doesn't exactly match, does it?"

Light illuminates. Light reveals. Light shows things for what they really are. So, shine the light of God's Word on your life and your marriage—or on your single life, for that matter. So wake up and turn on the light. Life is too short to sleepwalk through your days.

Wake Up

Ephesians 5:14 says: "Awake, you who sleep" (NKJV). In other words, get the sleep out of your eyes and the fog out of your mind. Be alert. Take action. Wake up to the reality of a culture that is hostile to the family and to your faith.

This is what the nation of Israel was guilty of so many times. They would worship God, they would follow Him, and then they would let their guard down. They'd get comfortable and begin to worship false idols, sacrificing to false gods. And what would happen? God would not accept it. He would send a wake-up call to get their attention.

It's the same thing with us. We get too comfortable with cultural norms and start going down roads we shouldn't. If we're too blind to see that we're blowing it, God might need to send a wake-up call.

Walk Carefully

Ephesians 5:15 says: "Walk circumspectly" (KJV).

This word speaks of something that is accurate and exact. It conveys the idea of examining or investigating something with great care. It is paying attention to detail. It reminds me of preparing to sign an important contract or document and how you want to be sure you read the fine print before you sign on the dotted line.

In the same way, if you want to have a successful marriage, read the fine print of what God's Word says. Don't say your vows until you're truly ready to live by them. Successful marriages aren't obtained by careless, random, or haphazard living. No, good marriages result when husbands and wives pay attention to detail, and carefully apply biblical principles to their lives. To be the husband, wife, father, or mother who God wants us to be, we must acknowledge our profound need of God's help through His strength, perspective, wisdom, and grace.

Redeem the Time (with God's Help)

Ephesians 5:16 says, "Redeeming the time, because the days are evil" (NKJV). The J. B. Phillips translation renders the verse as follows: "Make the best use of your time, despite all the difficulties of these days."

In other words, avoid frittering away your hours and days on worthless pursuits. Get your house in order, and get your life sorted out. As the prophet said to King Hezekiah, "Thus says the Lord: 'Set your house in order, for you shall die and not live'" (Isaiah 38:1 NKJV).

When you think about it, that's true of all of us. Each one of us will live out our brief lives on earth, and then stand before our Creator. Is your house in order? Is it what God wants it to be? You say, "It isn't easy to be a husband . . . or a wife . . . or a parent." That's true. But God will never ask you to do anything without providing you with the power to do so.

Think about how often your kids are willing to ask for help because they know there are things they can't do. They can't reach that top shelf, they can't make themselves a meal, they can't figure out their math assignment. They're free to come and ask you, and that's what we need to do with God. When getting our houses in order, instead of trying to fumble through it alone, let's ask God.

Be Filled with the Holy Spirit

Ephesians 5:18 reads: "Do not be drunk with wine, . . . but be filled with the Spirit" (NKJV).

In the verses following the passage above, we read that wives are to submit to their husbands, and husbands are to love their wives as Christ loved the church. But before a word is spoken about any of these things, God says, "Be filled with the Spirit."

Why?

Because we can't live an unselfish life or become an other-centered spouse apart from the direct empowerment of God's Holy Spirit. A husband cannot love his wife as Christ loves the church, and a wife cannot effectively submit to her husband as unto the Lord, without supernatural help and enabling.

Before a word is ever mentioned about the specific roles of the husband and wife in this vital chapter of Ephesians, God puts forth His prerequisite: "Be filled with the Spirit." In the original language, this statement is a command. God isn't saying, "Would you mind, as a personal favor to Me, if you have time, please, be filled with the Spirit." No, God is saying, "I command you to be filled with the Spirit."

There's another thing we need to know about the phrase *be filled with the Spirit*. It speaks of a continuous action. It could be translated from the Greek as "be constantly filled over and over again with the Holy Spirit."

Say you went out and bought a new car. You were told this car would run 100,000 miles easily, maybe even 200,000. "That's great," you think. So, you drive it off the lot, and run around town on your new wheels for a week or so with no problems. Then one day, it sputters and comes to a standstill. "That salesperson lied to me," you say to yourself. Then on your dashboard you notice a little red light and an arrow pointing to the letter E.

You're out of fuel. You don't need to take the car back and trade it in, and you don't need a new engine. You just need to go to a gas station and get a refill.

In the same way, your marriage can be humming along, things going great. Then all of the sudden, you find yourself chugging rather than humming. Maybe you've found yourself thinking, "It's my spouse. He [or she] isn't meeting my needs anymore. I think we've fallen out of love. I guess I need to trade this old model in for a new one."

No. You just need a refill. Did you know that God gives refills?

There's nothing complicated about it. You just pull in and say, "Lord, fill me with Your wonderful Holy Spirit. Fill me again." Each and every day you say, "Lord, I need to be empowered by and filled with Your Spirit. I am completely dependent on You."

This command speaks to life in its totality. But it also applies to the marriage relationship in particular. If you want to be the husband or wife God wants you to be, you need the power of the Holy Spirit in your life.

But what exactly does it mean to be "filled with the Spirit"?

Under His Control

The first thing we should note is that in the Greek, this verb be *filled* is in the imperative mode. What does that mean? It means we're talking about a command, not a suggestion! To fail to do so is to effectively cut off your power supply, and render you unable to be the spouse or parent God intends.

The verb in the Greek also speaks of a continuous action. A better translation would be, "Be *continuously* filled with the Holy Spirit." Let me add here that this may having nothing to do with your emotions. Many of us attach way too much emotional baggage to the filling of the Spirit. You don't have to weep and wail, tremble and shake, or even raise your voice. That's not what it means to be filled. Another way you could translate "be filled" is "be controlled" by the Spirit.

The Greek word speaks of wind filling a sail. So, there you are in your little sailboat out on a lake, and a gust of wind comes, filling your sails and moving you forward toward the desired destination. I love that imagery. There is power, beauty, and practicality in that picture of a wind-filled sail thrusting a boat forward through the waves. In the same way, God's Spirit wants to empower us, move us, guide us, and direct us.

But that Greek term translated "filled" could also mean "to permeate." It's the idea of salt permeating meat. Back when the New Testament was written, meat was preserved by rubbing salt deep into its fibers. This tells us that the Holy Spirit wants to permeate our lives, touching everything we think, do, and say, entering every fiber of our being.

So let the Holy Spirit fill your sails. Let the Holy Spirit permeate every area of your life. Let the Holy Spirit control you in all that you say and do. This is a clear command, and something you should do over and over again. To prepare your heart for dating, marriage, parenting, and even grandparenting, be filled with the Holy Spirit and remain under His control. He will never lead you astray.

Prayer: Lord, please help us build on Your foundation, choosing Your way above the world. Whether we're single, dating, or married, give us a willingness to do what Your Word says. We want to follow the wisdom of Ephesians 5 as we learn to walk in a new way, redeeming the time. Prepare our hearts by showing us Your will and way. We want to follow You in everything we do. Fill us continually with Your Spirit, empowering us with all the help in the universe to be the people You've called us to be. In Jesus' name, amen.

QUESTIONS for Discussion

1. Some marriages are built on money, fame, sexual attraction, and appearance. In contrast, some marriages are built on the solid rock of Christ. When reading Matthew 7:24–27, how does marriage stand a much better chance when built on rock instead of sinking sand? What are some ways you can reinforce your relationship now, to withstand the rains that come?

2. When we read, "The best thing that you could do is ask God to choose [a date] for you," how does that go against the cultural tide? Do you trust God enough to lead you to the right person at the right time?

3. We read, "If you pick a guy or girl thinking, 'I'm going to marry them and fix them,' don't marry them. Because here's reality, they may end up worse than they are now. Chances are, they're going to become a more exaggerated version of the person you see now." Does this

match up with what you believe? What are the possible consequences of marrying someone with the intention of fixing them or changing them in some way?

4. In this chapter, we read, "While you are dating, make it your goal to glorify God. Follow His plan and His will, rather than your desires and impulses. Seek to edify each other by building each other up, praying for each other, reading Scripture together, and calling each other to spiritual depth. These are ways to prepare your heart and your relationship as you are dating." How could following God's plan make all the difference in preparing your heart for marriage? What specific things are you implementing in your relationship that are building a solid foundation (praying together, reading Scripture, etc.)?

5. Ephesians 5:11 says, "Have no fellowship with the unfruitful works of darkness, but rather expose them" (NKJV). How do we handle a biblical directive like this in a culture that seems to value tolerance above all else?

6. When you read that light illuminates and reveals things, how does it encourage you to shine the light of God's Word on your life and marriage—or on your single life, for that matter? What would keep you from letting God's light expose what needs to be exposed? Pray into this, and let the light of Christ refine your relationships.

7. Quoting Ephesians 5:14, "Awake, you who sleep" (NKJV), we are encouraged to "get the sleep out of your eyes and the fog out of your mind. Be alert. Take action. Wake up to the reality of a culture that is hostile to the family and your faith." What causes that spiritual sleepiness and fog to come into our lives? What are its dangers? What steps can we take to be more alert to both the dangers and opportunities confronting our families?

8. The J. B. Phillips translation of Ephesians 5:16 says, "Make the best use of your time, despite all the difficulties of these days." Recognizing the danger to Christian marriages and families today, what steps can you and your spouse take to make better use of your available time?

9. We read these important words: "To fail [to be continuously filled with the Spirit] is to effectively cut off your power supply and render you unable to be the spouse or parent God intends." How are you continuously being filled with the Holy Spirit, relying on His strength to be the man or woman He's called you to be? How might we use this word picture to describe a Spirit-filled, Spirit-directed, Spirit-empowered marriage relationship?

10. Another meaning for the Greek term *be filled* could be translated "to permeate," like salt permeating meat in order to preserve it. We read, "This tells us that the Holy Spirit wants to permeate our lives, touching everything we think, do, and say, entering every fiber of our being." What might this say about God's desire to touch and influence every aspect of your life—with nothing held back?

CHAPTER 4

Submitting to Honor Christ

"Honor Christ by submitting to each other." —Ephesians 5:21 (TLB)

When Mattel first introduced Teen Talk Barbie in the 1990s, one of her many phrases triggered a great public outcry. Four little words generated such a public-relations dilemma for Mattel that Teen Talk Barbie had to be yanked from the market until she changed her tune. The offending remark?

"Math class is tough!"

If Ken had said that, no one would have even noticed. But as this Barbie inadvertently confirmed, there is a hypersensitivity in our culture regarding what a woman is or is not.

If ever there was a concept relating to women that was unpopular today, it would be the one we're about to look at in Scripture. Many would say the concepts found in the pages of the New Testament are outdated and archaic in our now-liberated society. Yes, they are old-fashioned to some, but to others, they are right on the cutting edge of life.

More importantly, biblical concepts and principles actually *work* in life. God's Word always makes a difference when it is heeded and applied. Why? Quite simply, because it's *true*.

As we look at the state of the American family in the 21st century, we can safely say that very reason it's falling apart is because we have strayed from God's standards. Not only have we strayed from the standards, but they are now openly mocked, belittled, and scorned.

I firmly believe the breakdown of the family can, to a great degree, be laid at the feet of men today, because the role of the man in the home is that of initiator and leader. Because men have largely failed to fulfill the responsibility God has given them, we see the ripple effects in the home, in wives, in children, and in society as a whole.

A Christian woman reading these words might readily nod her head, saying, "Yes, that's true. It's the failure of the men." But that conclusion will only take you so far, because marriage is a two-way street. While men have their part in the relationship, which God has clearly laid out in Scripture, God also calls His daughters to specific standards. And one of those standards is to submit to the leadership of her husband, as unto the Lord.

With all of these practical words of counsel and instruction as a backdrop, Paul turns to the particular issue of marriage, and the relationship between a husband and a wife submitting to one another in the fear of God.

Submission is an unpopular word in our culture, isn't it? We don't like the idea of submitting, do we? And yet this is a word that surfaces again and again in the pages of the Bible. So, why are we afraid to submit? Some might say, "Because I don't want anyone taking advantage of me. I have my rights, and I ought to have my say-so the same as anyone else."

When someone quotes Ephesians 5:22, about wives submitting to husbands, you will have people who say, "I don't agree with that."

But hold on.

Let's first make sure we actually understand what this verse means. In the previous verse we read, "Submitting to one another in the fear of God."

Then, after setting that context, we read: "Wives, submit to your own husbands, as to the Lord. For the husband is head of the wife, as also Christ is head of the church; and He is the Savior of the body. Therefore, just as the church is subject to Christ, so let the wives be to their own husbands in everything" (verses 22–24 NKJV).

Supporting One Another

Not only are wives to submit to husbands, but husbands are to submit to their wives as well. Why? Because the first command here is "Honor Christ by submitting to each other" (verse 21 TLB).

What does this actually mean? To *submit* means "to get in order under something." It's sometimes used in a military sense, meaning "to rank beneath." For instance, in the military you have different ranks—general, colonel, first lieutenant, and so forth. There is a chain of command in the military, and a chain of command in life as well.

So, here's what this passage is saying. A husband's submission to his wife does not mean he abdicates his responsibility of leadership in the home. But it *does* mean that it helps her to bear her burdens. You could also translate this verse as "supporting one another in the fear of God."

He supports her by getting underneath her to help carry her burdens. He remains ready to sacrifice his own desires to meet her needs. And she is willing to do the same for him.

Another way to say it? *Put the needs of your mate above your own.*

Romans 12:10–12 teaches us to "love each other with genuine affection, and take delight in honoring each other. Never be lazy, but work hard and serve the Lord enthusiastically. Rejoice in our confident hope. Be patient in trouble, and keep on praying" (NLT).

These are great words from the apostle Paul, but what does it mean for our marriage? The main thing that jumps out at me is *humility*. We're to have humility, not thinking too highly of ourselves, but also, not thinking too lowly of ourselves.

Imagine a married person saying something like this: "I want this marriage to be about my spouse, not about me. I want to make my wife the happiest woman who ever lived." Or "I want to make my husband the happiest man in the world."

Do you know how this kind of humility, this sort of mindset, would change your entire marriage? But most couples think, "That isn't natural to us." And you know what? You're right. In fact, it's *supernatural.*

It takes the power and presence of God to accomplish humble submission toward our spouse. Paul tells us to imitate God and walk in love, but we need the indwelling presence of the Holy Spirit enabling us to follow that path day by day, moment by moment.

Far too often we make marriage about "me" and "my needs."

How can she fulfill me?

How can he make me a happier person?

What can he/she do for me?

When you live with the "It's all about me" mentality, it's draining. But when you switch your approach and empty yourself, you realize it is exactly what God wants so He can fill you up. When you empty yourself of your expectations and what you're hoping to get out of the marriage, and instead, open yourself up to what God has for you, it completely changes everything.

These days, we see all sorts of dating apps and matchmaking sites offering assistance to people who hope to find the right person. But as we've said before, a successful marriage isn't so much about finding the right person as much as it is about BEING the right person.

There is no perfect person out there, no matter how many identical boxes both of you might check on some online survey. It's about your being willing to change and adapt for the sake of your spouse. Philippians 2:4–6 says, "Don't just think about your own affairs, but be interested in others, too, and in what they are doing. Your attitude should be the kind that was shown us by Jesus Christ, who, though he was God, did not demand and cling to his rights as God" (TLB).

Another Scripture that undergirds the idea of mutual submission is 1 Corinthians 7:3–4, where the apostle Paul is speaking about sexual relations. He writes, "The husband should fulfill his wife's sexual needs, and the wife should fulfill her husband's needs. The wife gives authority over her body to her husband, and the husband gives authority over his body to his wife" (NLT).

Do you see Paul's point here? The husband no more possesses his wife than she possesses him. He is not superior; she is not inferior. And vice versa. *They belong to one another.* Paul is saying, "Her body belongs to you, and your body belongs to her. So don't deprive each other sexually unless you have agreed to this for a specific purpose and for a limited amount of time."

Here, once again, is the kernel of this teaching: You belong to one another. You support one another. You submit to one another. You help one another. *The two of you have become one.* In no way does the Bible teach that man is better than woman, or even above woman. We stand before God on equal ground. Galatians 3:28 says that in Christ "there is neither Jew nor Greek, there is neither slave nor free, there is neither male nor female" (NKJV). We are one in Jesus.

But even though there is no difference between man and woman in the nature of their salvation or standing with God, there is a principle of authority in the family. Those who struggle with the concept of the husband being the head of the home might be helped by considering Paul's words in 1 Corinthians 11:3: "I want you to realize that the head of every man is Christ, and the head of the woman is man, and the head of Christ is God" (NIV).

What does it mean that "the head of Christ is God"? The Bible speaks of a Trinity: Father, Son, and Holy Spirit. One is not better than the other. They are the same in nature and essence. At the same time, however, we read in Scripture that the Son submits to the Father and not because the Son is in any sense less than the Father. We see this played out beautifully in the Lord's life on earth, where He constantly submitted to the Father, called on the Father, and prayed to the Father. Yet Jesus Christ is Himself God incarnate, and the Holy Spirit is God as well.

Paul, then, is saying that the relationship structure of Jesus Christ to God the Father is the same as the relationship structure in marriage. Though the husband and wife are equal in their standing before God, in order for the family to function in harmony, the woman (with no loss of dignity) takes a place of submission to the leadership of her husband. God's divine design intends that her respect, help, and obedience will be matched by his servant leadership as they submit together to the Lord Jesus Christ and to each other.

Any guy with half a brain knows that marriage is a *partnership*, and he doesn't try to run the home like a banana-republic dictator. That's not what it means to lead. Biblical leadership is servant leadership. It is to lead as Jesus led.

If a man has to beat his chest and yell, "I am the head of this home, and you do what I tell you to do," something is very, very wrong. If he has true authority, he won't have to resort to screaming and pounding on walls.

No, he will have his wife's love and respect, and his leadership will be a natural result.

The Motive of Submission

Some might believe there's an ulterior motive to submission, but that's simply not true. Remember, Ephesians 5:22 says, "Wives, submit to your own husbands, as to the Lord" (NKJV).

In other words, wives submitting to their husbands is an act of submission to Jesus Christ Himself. As Colossians 3:23 says, "Whatever you do, work at it with all your heart, as working for the Lord, not for human masters" (NIV). Submission is brought into the best perspective when we see it as a heart offering to the Lord, something we do in honor of Him. Amen?

I remember years ago visiting the home of Ruth and Billy Graham. Ruth, now with the Lord, was a wonderful woman of God—and one of the most fun-loving people I've ever met. She was quick to laugh with a twinkle in her eye, but a true student of the Bible as well.

The day we visited, Ruth made lunch for us, and then washed the dishes by hand. I couldn't help noticing the sign over her sink that read: "Divine service done here three times a day." I was so impressed by that; she did even the small tasks of life as unto the Lord.

And so can you and I!

You can do anything "as unto the Lord." Whether you're a doctor, song-writer, gardener, or a hamburger flipper, "Whatever you do, put your whole heart and soul into it, as into work done for God, and not merely for men" (Colossians 3:23 PHI).

My wife, Cathe, describes it this way:

> There's beauty in submission. You are reflecting the role of Christ, and there is no demeaning of that. As a matter of fact, it's an exalted role. "Let him who is the greatest among you, be the servant of all." When you start to feel like a servant, just say to yourself, "I am playing out the role of Jesus in this. I am serving." And let me tell you, your husband will see it, and the Lord will see it, and there will be a blessed life.

I think that's the heart of this instruction to wives. Submit as unto Jesus Christ. Do it for Him, in honor and reverence of Him, as the Lord and Savior of your life. If you have difficulty submitting to your husband, then submit to God's Son, who loves you and died for you. Don't just do it for your husband; do it as though Jesus Himself asked it of you.

The Model of Submission

In Ephesians 5:23–24 we read: "For the husband is head of the wife, as also Christ is head of the church; and He is the Savior of the body. Therefore, just as the church is subject to Christ, so let the wives be to their own husbands in everything" (NKJV).

The ultimate model of submission is Jesus Christ, who laid down His privileges and rights, and ultimately His life—for us. In John 13, the Bible tells us how Jesus took off His outer garment, got down on His hands and knees, and washed the dirty feet of His disciples. He is our model for submission. Here's the account from John 13:3–5 (NLT):

> Jesus knew that the Father had given him authority over everything and that he had come from God and would return to God. So he got up from the table, took off his robe, wrapped a towel around his waist, and poured water into a basin. Then he began to wash the disciples' feet, drying them with the towel he had around him.

Did you catch that? Jesus had been given authority over everything, and I mean everything. Yet He was humble and submissive enough to wash the feet of His friends. His attitude was one of servitude, the perfect model for submission in marriage.

The Limits of Submission

Now, here's where it gets interesting. Does a Christian wife have to do everything her husband says, no matter what? No, that's not what the Bible teaches. A wife's submission—as well as a husband's—should first be to God.

First Peter 2:13–14 reads, "Submit yourselves for the Lord's sake to every human authority: whether to the emperor, as the supreme authority, or to governors, who are sent by him to punish those who do wrong and to commend those who do right" (NIV).

That, of course, means I should obey the laws of the land and pay my taxes. As citizens and believers, we have to obey these laws. That's the way our country works. Authority has been instituted by God, and we must respect it. But what if that same government passed a law tomorrow that said no one can pray to God anymore?

Daniel was presented with this exact quandary when the king of the Persian Empire signed a law that no one could pray to any god except the king himself. What did Daniel do? The Bible tells us that he continued to pray to the Lord, just as he always had. He didn't change his practice at all.

There comes a point where the law of God supersedes the law of man. What if the government passes a law that says we can't preach the gospel anymore? Do we shut everything down? No, we go on preaching and teaching just as we always have. When the apostles were told by the authorities that they could no longer preach in the name of Jesus, they said, "We ought to obey God rather than men" (Acts 5:29 NKJV).

Let's apply this principle to marriage. Say the husband is a nonbeliever, and you are the sweet, godly, Christian wife. Somehow, he learns about the biblical principle of submission, and he kind of likes that idea. So he says to his wife, "Why don't you submit to me while we go out drinking tonight?" or "Why don't you submit to me while I ask you to do this immoral thing right now?"

Do you submit? No, because there is a higher law at that point. If your husband asks you to do something that is against God's law, you are not to submit. On the other hand, if what your husband is asking you to do doesn't violate any of God's commands, you submit to the best of your ability.

Without a Word

"Wait a second," some wives are saying. "The Bible also says, 'Husbands, love your wives, just as Christ loved the church.'"

They think that if their husband isn't loving them as Christ loved the church, then they must not be obligated to submit. After all, if the man is the initiator, the one who should be taking the lead but is failing to do that, why should the woman be obligated to uphold her end of the bargain?

First Peter chapter 3, however, contradicts this thinking:

> Wives, likewise, be submissive to your own husbands, that even if some do not obey the word, they, without a word, may be won by the conduct of their wives, when they observe your chaste conduct accompanied by fear. Do not let your adornment be merely outward—arranging the hair, wearing gold, or putting on fine apparel—rather let it be the hidden person of the heart, with the incorruptible beauty of a gentle and quiet spirit, which is very precious in the sight of God. For in this manner, in former times, the holy women who trusted in God also adorned themselves, being submissive to their own husbands, as Sarah obeyed Abraham, calling him lord, whose daughters you are if you do good and are not afraid with any terror. (verses 1–6 NKJV)

This passage deals with a Christian woman who is married to a non-Christian man and what she can do to reach her husband for Christ. I also believe these verses apply to a Christian woman who is married to a nominally Christian man, or a man who may name the name of Christ, but has not stepped up into the role of spiritual leader. God has given wives a positive strategy to follow in reaching their husbands, and clearly lays out the role and responsibilities of the Christian wife in the marriage relationship. In fact, as a wife begins to apply the principles found here, she might even see her husband become a new-and-improved model.

The strategy for reaching your husband, Peter says, is "without a word." Here is a man who is an unbeliever, and his wife wants him to come to faith. She might think, "Maybe I should just hit him with a sermon every single day. I'll stuff gospel tracts into his shirt pockets. When he comes home from work, I'll preach to him. I'll make him watch Christian TV programs with me."

Although there is a place for declaring the Word, there is also a place for *living* it. What you need to do is let God reach him by the Holy Spirit, as you live out your radiant, Spirit-filled, Christ-fragrant life.

What if you're married to an unbeliever? Sadly, this happens all too often to single Christian women who get tired of waiting on God and waiting for a Christian Mr. Right, and instead marry some man who is not a follower of Jesus Christ. Somehow, they think the verse that says "do not be unequally yoked together with unbelievers" (2 Corinthians 6:14) doesn't apply to them. But then some time passes, and they are miserable in that relationship.

I have even had some of these women over the years come to me and say, "I've met this really great Christian man at church. God has told me that I can divorce my non-Christian husband and marry this Christian guy." And I've heard it the other way around, too. Christian guys have come to me and said, "God has told me that I can divorce my non-Christian wife and marry this great Christian woman." My reply to that is "No, He didn't." I can guarantee that God *did not* tell them this, because 1 Corinthians 7:13 says, "And a woman who has a husband who does not believe, if he is willing to live with her, let her not divorce him" (NKJV).

That sounds pretty clear to me. We also read in 1 Corinthians 7:27, "Are you bound to a wife? Do not seek to be loosed. Are you loosed from a wife? Do not seek a wife" (NKJV).

So, believers who are married to unbelievers should stick with that commitment and pray that the unbelieving spouse will come to his or her senses and come to the Lord.

How will that happen? More often than not it will come about because of how you live, more than what you say. Live a godly life, and God will do the saving.

No Nagging or Manipulating

Telling a woman that the way to reach her husband is by *not saying any-thing* is one of the most difficult things you could ask. Women, by nature, are very verbal, and gifted by the Creator with the ability to persuade. If this gift is yielded for good to God, it can have a profound influence. But if it is yielded for evil to Satan, it can be destructive.

For example, consider how Esther was able to use her feminine influence to rescue a whole generation of Jewish people. Then look at how Eve misused her feminine influence to move her husband in the wrong direction. Of course, Adam was responsible for what he did, but she helped facilitate the process.

You see, what wives must avoid is manipulation: trying to do things that would move her husband to do what she wants him to do. Manipulation can be defined as "managing or influencing by artful or devious skill."

Wives must avoid this temptation to manipulate because it will never bring about lasting change. I know it's tempting when he doesn't seem to be listening. You want to help out God a little bit, so you think,

> I'll just weld the knob on the radio to a Christian station and then crank the volume all the way up.

> I'll put little gospel tracts in his sandwiches. Instead of turkey, it will be "The Four Spiritual Laws."

> I'll get Christian guys to seek him out and try to talk to him.

Most likely, he will see through all of that. He will know what you're trying to do, and may very well rebel from it. It will drive him away instead of drawing him in. Attempting to nag him into the kingdom will not have the effect you were hoping for.

Solomon, who had many, many wives and knew a little bit about nagging, had this to say in Proverbs 27:15: "A quarrelsome wife is as annoying as constant dripping on a rainy day" (NLT). He also observed in Proverbs 21:19, "It's better to live alone in the desert than with a quarrelsome, complaining wife."

Women nag when their husbands don't seem to be paying attention to them, so they keep pressing the point until hopefully he gets the message. But the fact of the matter is that nagging doesn't reach a man. Actually, it drives him away.

It's very easy to only pick up on the negatives in a marriage relationship. "You didn't take out the trash. Why don't you clean the toothpaste off the mirror? You didn't wash your whiskers down the sink. You left your tools out when you were working on the car. When are you going to fix this?"

Is that all he's hearing about? What's *wrong* in your home and in your marriage? He also needs to hear about what's *right*. He needs to hear that you appreciate him, that you love him, and that you find him attractive. Don't assume that men are so self-assured that they don't need to hear these things. They do. Maybe a lot. They need to be encouraged and reassured.

One reason a man often gets involved with another woman is because someone will come along and pay attention to him and tell him he is so special and so wonderful. Then he goes home and perhaps never hears that from his wife. He even wonders at times if his wife still loves him. Wives need to verbally communicate their affection and appreciation to their husbands.

But the primary concept of the idea of winning your husband without a word is what could be described as "the silent preaching of a lovely life."[6] It is to first prepare the ground of his heart by living out your faith in the home. If you fail to do this, he will never listen to your message and will actually have an excuse for his unbelief. But on the other hand, if you break up the soil of his heart with your actions, your words will have far greater impact, and will eventually take root.

This same principle could be applied to other people in our lives whom we want to win to Christ, be it parents, children, friends, or coworkers. They don't need a sermon every day. They've heard your message. Now live it. Show yourself to be a Christian in practical, tangible ways, and that will open their hearts to the seed of the Word of God. They will see a distinct difference in your lifestyle as a result of your knowing Jesus Christ. That will speak volumes to them. A quote often attributed to Saint Francis of Assisi says, "Preach the Gospel, and when necessary, use words."[7]

Jesus told us that we are to be the salt of the earth and the light of the world (see Matthew 5:13–14). Many of us are light without being salt, and sometimes we are salt without being light. Being light without being salt means that we talk about our faith all the time. We proclaim it, but we aren't really living it.

Being salt means that we're having an effect on people around us, but maybe we're not talking about our faith as much as we should. There is a place for both salt and light. There is a place for testimony and speaking for Christ and a place for living the life. Both go hand in hand, and it's a powerful combination when it is empowered by God's Holy Spirit.

Looking Good

Returning to 1 Peter 3, we come to the subject of a Christian woman's outward appearance:

> Do not let your adornment be merely outward—arranging the hair, wearing gold, or putting on fine apparel—rather let it be the hidden person of the heart, with the incorruptible beauty of a gentle and quiet spirit, which is very precious in the sight of God. For in this manner, in former times, the holy women who trusted in God also adorned themselves, being submissive to their own husbands. (verses 3–5 NKJV)

The word "adornment," used here, comes from the Greek word *cosmos*, from which we get the English word "cosmetic." Peter is talking about the emptiness of focusing on the outside while ignoring the inside.

As we look at this passage, it helps to understand the culture of the time. Roman women were given over to the latest fashion crazes, and were very focused on their looks. In fact, some of the engravings from this era indicate that women wore towering hairdos with nets of gold and expensive combs. They also wore gold rings and bracelets around their necks, ankles, and arms. As a result, they would invest a great deal of time each day to their outward appearance.

Peter was essentially saying, "Bring this into balance. Don't flaunt your outward looks or make it your primary focus. Work on the attractiveness of your inner person as well." The phrase "putting on fine apparel" isn't saying that it's wrong for a Christian woman to be fashion-conscious or attractive.

Peter's point is simply this: Don't let clothing become your main focus in life. In fact, "putting on fine apparel" could be translated as "the frequent changing of clothing." It conveys the idea of a woman who is constantly changing her clothes for the purpose of impressing people. She wants everyone to notice how great she looks. Peter was saying, "Focus instead on the inner person. Think about the inside."

When it comes to this passage in Scripture, I'm sometimes asked, "What do you think about makeup? Should a woman wear makeup?" In answer to that, I quote Charles Swindoll: "Does [a house] need painting? Paint it!"[8]

Nevertheless, all of us, and especially women, need to be concerned with the *inside* of the house as well as the outside, because the inside is what really matters. This is what's really being addressed here. In the description of the virtuous wife in Proverbs 31, we are told that she is aware of her outward appearance. She goes about her work with vigor and strengthens her arms. I don't know if she did arm curls or if they had Hebrew aerobics back then. But she is a woman who cares about the way she looks. In other words, a wife shouldn't go to the opposite extreme and neglect her appearance, either.

We hear the verse, "For bodily exercise profits a little" (1 Timothy 4:8 NKJV), which is often quoted by overweight or out-of-shape people. While it's true that bodily exercise profits only "a little," at least it does profit *some*. The remainder of the verse says, "But godliness is profitable for all things, having promise of the life that now is and of that which is to come."

Think of it as temple maintenance. Your body is the temple of the Holy Spirit, and you should do what you can as a Christian woman to continue to be outwardly attractive to your husband. Even so, you should not do it at the expense of inward beauty.

Inner beauty is a very appealing quality that a Christian woman develops over the years. It is not achieved with makeup or clothes. Rather, it's a glow and a radiance that shines from the inside out.

What a marvelous quality this is in a godly woman. This is what 1 Peter 3:4 is speaking of: "Let it be the hidden person of the heart, with the incorruptible beauty of a gentle and quiet spirit, which is very precious in the sight of God" (NKJV). Or as another translation puts it, "The unfading loveliness of a calm and gentle spirit" (PHI).

Referring to "the hidden person of the heart," this phrase doesn't mean that a wife must sit around in silence and can't disagree with her husband or offer a different opinion. She certainly should speak her mind, and try to influence her husband for good. I would even venture to say that she has a God-given right and responsibility to set her husband straight if he's off course.

I have come to highly value and respect my wife's opinions over the years. She has a way of seeing through a situation. I find that she often has discernment and observations about people that I might otherwise miss or overlook. She provides insight and wisdom, and that is virtue.

Don't Just Love Him, Like Him

Finally, I want to point out that when the Scripture says that wives are to love their husbands, the word used for "love" in the original language is the Greek word *phileo*. It is one of several words for love in the Greek language.

It refers to a friendship love. It is a given that wives should *agape* their husbands, which is a sacrificial, spiritual love. Yet wives are to *phileo* their husbands as well. Loosely translated, "Wives, *like* your husbands."

Don't just love him. Like him, and let him know. Reassure him. He needs to hear that from you. And, let him lead—even if he doesn't do it perfectly. Let him make a few mistakes, but strengthen him in that leadership role, and don't undermine it by being overly critical or sarcastic. Don't try to make his leadership role difficult for him. Instead, make it easier. It's a lot of responsibility to bear, and it's not as easy as you might think.

Your husband needs your prayers, your support, and your encouragement. He needs to hear your commitment to him and your love for him reaffirmed.

So, wives, submit to your husbands as to the Lord and win him without a word. Concentrate on the beauty of your inner person, even while maintaining an attractive outer appearance. How true it is when Scripture says, "Charm is deceitful and beauty is passing, but a woman who fears the Lord, she shall be praised" (Proverbs 31:30 NKJV).

Concentrate on the responsibilities God has given to you, and by the power of His Spirit, He will help you to be the woman He wants you to be.

If you are a husband reading this today and have, by God's grace, found yourself married to such a woman, don't take it for granted! Proverbs 18:22 says, "He who finds a wife finds a good thing, and obtains favor from the LORD" (NKJV). If you have found a godly woman who is dedicated to Jesus Christ and has made a commitment to you, then you have a treasure of greater value than everything else on earth.

Prayer: Lord, You gave us the word "submission," not to cause conflict, but to bring unity. Please help us understand this concept better, as we trust Your standard for marriage. Father, draw us into the oneness You desire, first with You, then with each other. Help us lay down all resistance to submission, gratefully stepping into the roles for which You created us. Tune out the voices of the culture that have turned submission into an ugly word, and instead, tune our hearts to Your beautiful truth. In Jesus' name, amen.

QUESTIONS for Discussion

1. How does the verse "submitting to one another in the fear of God" (Ephesians 5:21 NKJV) set the context for the specific instructions to wives and husbands that follow in verses 22–30? How can you view this as a way of "submitting to one another"?

2. Referring again to Ephesians 5:21, this chapter said, "A husband's submission to his wife does not mean he abdicates his responsibility

of leadership in the home. But it does mean that it helps her to bear her burdens." What does a husband's God-honoring submission to his wife look like in everyday life? Why is this sort of submission no danger to his responsibility of leadership?

3. Romans 12:10–12 teaches us to, "love each other with genuine affection, and take delight in honoring each other. Never be lazy, but work hard and serve the Lord enthusiastically. Rejoice in our confident hope, be patient in trouble, and keep on praying" (NLT). How does this passage emphasize humility in your approach to submission? How does it change your attitude from begrudgingly serving your spouse, to lovingly serving your spouse?

4. To those who struggle with the concept of the husband being the head of the home, Paul says in 1 Corinthians 11:3, "But I want you to realize that the head of every man is Christ, and the head of the woman is man, and the head of Christ is God" (NIV). What do we learn from this passage? What does the submission of Jesus Christ to the Father tell us or illustrate for us about the submission of a wife to her husband?

5. Referring to the leadership of the husband in a marriage, this chapter stated that "biblical leadership is servant leadership." What are some of the characteristics of a leader who is also a servant? Why is that kind of leadership easier to respond to?

6. Ephesians 5:22 reads: "Wives, submit to your own husbands, as to the Lord" (NKJV). How might those last four words impact a wife's desire and motivation to follow this biblical imperative? Lay this Scripture alongside Colossians 3:23. What parallels do you see between the two?

7. What is the responsibility of a wife whose husband asks her to submit to something immoral or illegal? How does the account in Acts 5:27–29 help us to gain perspective on this?

8. The strategy for wives reaching their husbands is, as Peter says, "without a word." How difficult is this concept in your marriage? What would it look like to let your actions speak louder than your words?

9. When this chapter talked about the "emptiness" of focusing on your outer appearance, but neglecting what's on the inside, how did that resonate with you? How can you take good care of the "temple" God gave you—inside and out?

10. Wives are to *phileo* their husbands, which means to "like" them. In what specific ways are you telling or showing your husband that you like (enjoy) him? And husbands, how are you openly appreciating the wonderful wife you've been given? As Proverbs 18:22 says, "He who finds a wife finds a good thing, and obtains favor from the LORD" (NKJV).

CHAPTER 5

Four Words That Can Change a Marriage

*"Therefore do not be unwise, but understand
what the will of the Lord is."* —Ephesians 5:17 (NKJV)

A man was walking along a Southern California beach and spotted an unusual-looking bronze object laying in the sand. He picked it up and began to dust it off, when all of a sudden, a genie appeared.

The genie told him, "Master, I will grant you one wish."

"One wish?" the man asked. "What happened to three wishes?"

The genie said, "We've had some recent budget cuts. We can only do one wish."

"Wow, that's a hard one," said the man.

He thought for a minute, then said, "I love Hawaii, but I don't like to fly. If you could build me a highway from California to Hawaii so that I could drive there, that would be great. So that's my one wish. I want a highway from California to Hawaii."

"Give me a break!" the genie exclaimed. "There's no way I could do that! Didn't I just tell you that we are on a budget? It's absolutely impossible. You'll need to choose something else."

The man thought about it again. "Okay," he said quietly. "I think I have it now. I don't understand women at all, especially my wife. My wish is that I would be able to understand women from this point forward."

The genie turned away for a moment, seemingly deep in thought. Then he turned back to the man and said, "Do you want that highway with two lanes or four?"

I wish I could share with you the magic key to understanding your wife, but having been married for more than 50 years, I can honestly say I'm still a long way from that goal. Even though we husbands might have a hard time understanding our wives sometimes, we are still directed to love them (and really, they can be so lovable).

Every marriage, however, will face difficulties and challenges—even good marriages. In fact, sometimes this is what makes a good marriage. As we come through those difficulties, we learn how to bend, to flex, and most importantly, how to love and forgive.

But we need to ask ourselves, "Am I, as a husband, doing my part in the marriage?" The question is not whether your wife is doing her part. *Put that question out of your mind.* The real issue is, are you doing yours? A failure to understand and apply the specific roles and responsibilities given to the husband and wife is the reason for the breakdown of so many marriages today.

Do you know what your responsibilities are? Scripture is actually quite clear on the subject. In fact, I'll venture to say that the bulk of the responsibility for the success of the marriage, in my opinion, rests squarely on the man's shoulders.

The truth is that many of us aren't being the leaders we ought to be. As a result, countless marriages are in trouble today because men are unwilling to obey God's specific commands.

So, what are these commands? I'll list a few of them from Ephesians 5:25–33, but first, let's read the whole passage:

> Husbands, love your wives, just as Christ also loved the church and gave Himself for her, that He might sanctify and cleanse her

with the washing of water by the word, that He might present her to Himself a glorious church, not having spot or wrinkle or any such thing, but that she should be holy and without blemish. So husbands ought to love their own wives as their own bodies; he who loves his wife loves himself. For no one ever hated his own flesh, but nourishes and cherishes it, just as the Lord does the church. For we are members of His body, of His flesh and of His bones. "For this reason a man shall leave his father and mother and be joined to his wife, and the two shall become one flesh." This is a great mystery, but I speak concerning Christ and the church. Nevertheless let each one of you in particular so love his own wife as himself, and let the wife see that she respects her husband. (NKJV)

Now, let's break it down:

Husbands, love your wives, just as Christ also loved the church and gave Himself for her.

Sanctify and cleanse her with the washing of water by the word.

Leave your father and mother and be joined to your wife. You are one flesh.

Husbands, love your own wife as yourself.

So often we try to complicate things, don't we? But the commands Paul shares in this passage are direct and to the point. And it all starts with one key principle.

Change Your Marriage with These Four Words

Here, then, are the four words that can change your marriage: "Husbands, love your wives."

If husbands would man up and do what God calls them to do, what a difference it would make in the church, in our world, in our culture. But here's the problem: Even at our best, we men are prone to fall into a pattern of passivity. And at our worst, we're dragging everyone else down with us. There are far too many situations where the man in the house is either indifferent to the things of the Lord, or is an active hindrance to the rest of his family in their search for God.

Passivity in a Christian man is tragic. This is a man who is simply going through the motions in his walk with Christ, and has lost the fire and desire he once had.

"Oh sure, we can go to church," he might say. "But I'd really rather watch the game on TV."

Come on, get up and be a man! *Lead* your wife. *Lead* your children. Show them what a man of God looks like. This is the gauntlet Paul throws down here in Ephesians 5.

I heard a story about a husband and wife who got up one morning before church. It was about time to walk out the door, and the wife saw that her husband was still in his pajamas lying in bed, so she said, "Sweetie, come on. We do this every week. It's time to get up and go to church. You need to get ready; you need to get dressed. Come on. Time is ticking."

And he responded, "Well, sweetie, you know what? I'll give you three reasons why I'm not going to church today. Number one, the church is cold. Number two, nobody likes me. And number three, I'm just not going."

To which the wife replied, "Wow, okay. Well, I'll give you three reasons why you should go to church. Number one, the church is not cold, number two, people like you there, and number three, you're the pastor, so get up and get dressed. We're going."

Loving is leading. When husbands refuse to lead, they put their wives in positions they were never meant to fulfill. This doesn't mean women can't lead others well. They can and do. But husbands have a biblical responsibility to lead, and it falls under the umbrella of loving your wife as Christ loves the church.

Did you know that 90 percent of the books sold on the topic of marriage and family are purchased by women?[9] The women are out there buying the books, trying to find out how to follow the Lord and be better wives. And the guys? Well, too many of us are flipping through the channels, overly preoccupied with work, or neck-deep in fishing, football or some other hobby.

The fact is, 70 to 80 percent of Christian books in general are bought by women.[10] What's up with that? Don't men need to learn? Don't men need to grow? Of course we do. And we need to love our wives by leading the way in the Christian life.

> Jonathan's Thoughts: Listen, there are two things in life that I felt like I was pretty prepared for. As I approached them, I felt like I had a good grasp on things. I felt like I would have a good handle on them, and be able to take care of them better than I actually could. Can you guess what those two things were?
>
> Marriage and parenting.
>
> "Husbands, love your wives as Christ loves the church." I felt pretty good thinking, "Oh, yeah, I got that. That's good. No worries there."
>
> "Husbands, love your wives. Wives, respect your husbands." I thought, "Cool, cool. I got this." But you know what? I had no idea what this would require.

Take a Second Look at "Love"

Someone might say, "Paul says to love my wife. What's so difficult about that?" First, you'd better understand a little about the Greek word Paul uses for *love* here.

In our English language, we basically have one word for *love*. We use it to describe everything from "I love my dog" to "I love golf" to "I love my wife." Yet in Greek, the original language of the New Testament, there are several words for "love."

There is *eros*, which primarily refers to love on the physical plane. This is where our English word "erotic" comes from.

There is *phileo*, which is love on the emotional plane. The name "Philadelphia," meaning "house of brotherly love," derives from *phileo*. There is *storge*, which refers to family love, as in the love for parents or children. Then there is *agape*, which speaks of a sacrificial, spiritual love.

This last word for love is a radical, self-giving, all-consuming love. It's the word used more often than any other in the Gospels to describe the love of God Himself. In John 3:16 we read, "For God so [*agaped*] the world that He gave His only begotten Son" (NKJV).

This is not to say that *eros*, and even *phileo*, don't have a part to play in a marriage. When you first saw your wife, you most likely found her physically attractive. So *eros* does play a part. Yet we tend to equate the word "erotic" with evil, because it's usually presented in a twisted and perverted manner. But *eros* is a God-given love, and in its proper place, it has the blessing of the Lord.

Of course, that proper place is within the parameters and safety of the marriage relationship . . . *and nowhere else.* The sexual union between a husband and wife is a way to express their intimacy, their oneness with each other, and of course, for the purpose of bearing children. But it is something that God designed uniquely for a man and a woman who are committed in marriage to enjoy. The problem with *eros* is that it's essentially selfish. *Eros* basically says, "I want something from you. Give it to me now." While *eros* has its place, you can't build a marriage on it.

Then there's *phileo*. In many ways, *phileo* is a more noble love than eros, because *phileo* is a give-and-take love. It's really a love that says, "I love you if you love me," or "I love you as long as I find something lovable in you." Phileo is a love that expects something back—and springs from the sense of pleasure we draw from the object or the person loved. You feel good when you're with that person. He or she is fun to be with, makes you laugh, or entertains you. You love that person because of what he or she brings to the relationship, and you are loved for the same reason.

This world's love is primarily object-oriented. A person is loved because of their physical attractiveness, personality, wit, prestige, talent, or some other feature or trait we happen to find appealing. We love someone because they made it into *People* magazine's "50 Most Beautiful People" issue. Or we love the way they sing. We love the way they write. We love the way they do this or that. The problem is that this is a fickle kind of love. If the trait we find lovable—like beauty, for example—is diminished by age, or if someone more talented or gifted comes along, then this fickle love is transferred.

Here's the problem: Many people enter into marriage with nothing more than *eros* and *phileo*. They inwardly think: "I will love you as long as you are attractive to me, appealing to me, and I find what I want from you. But the moment you cease to do that for me, I'm moving on. I don't want you in my life anymore."

The marriage is then dissolved because of so-called irreconcilable differences. (There's that ridiculous phrase!)

In contrast to *eros* and *phileo*, *agape* springs from a sense of the preciousness of the object being loved. *Agape* is primarily determined by the character of the one who loves, and not necessarily whether the object is lovable. *Agape* is not a mere feeling or emotion. It is far more. This is the kind of love God commands us to have as husbands.

God commands us to love our wives with *agape*—not with a fickle love dependent upon her day-to-day lovability. *Agape* loves in spite of all that. This is a love that transforms the one being loved. As you love your wife like this, it will change her, just as Christ loved you like this, and it changed you.

The husband who loves his wife for what she can give him loves as the world loves, and not as Christ loves. But the husband who loves his wife as Christ loves the church gives everything he has for his wife, including his own life, if necessary.

If a loving husband is willing to sacrifice his own life for his wife, then how much more should he be willing to make lesser sacrifices for her, such as his own likes and dislikes, desires, opinions, preferences, and personal welfare? How much more should he be willing to set these aside to please her and meet her needs? He dies to self in order to live for his wife, because this is what Christ's love demands.

So instead of lecturing your wife on what she is supposed to do, why don't you look at what *you're* supposed to do? Make sure you are loving your wife as Christ loved the church.

Just Do It

Husbands, *agape* your wives.

Get after it. It's your mission, and God's clear command.

It's not just being "pleasant" or "nice" (though that's a good place to start). Rather, it is a deep affection and involvement, even if the object of that love seems unlovable at times.

"But she drives me crazy sometimes."

All right. So what?

"Well, it's really hard, because I don't find her attractive anymore. I did think she was attractive once, but she isn't anymore."

What does that have to do with it?

You need to love her as Christ loves the church, and you need to let her know that you love her.

I heard about a couple that was struggling, so they went to see a marriage counselor. After listening to the wife and the husband for a while, the counselor got up from his chair, came around to the front of his desk, and asked the wife to stand up. When she stood up, he put his arms around her and gave her a good hug.

"This," he said to the husband, "is what your wife needs every single day from now on."

The husband replied, "What time do you want me to bring her back tomorrow?"

When was the last time you hugged your wife, without angling to get anything else? When is the last time you told her she's beautiful? It really doesn't do much good to *think* it, because she can't read your mind. You actually have to tell her, saying the words.

You say, "Well, the romance is gone in our marriage."

Then get it back.

Do what you did for her in the early days of your relationship. Set about winning her love and affection all over again. Don't wait for some random surge of emotion to get started—*just do it*, to borrow a popular phrase.

How about going on a date together? (And probably not to a cage fight or a demolition derby.) How about doing those simple things like opening a door for her, complimenting her, or buying some little gift for her? Don't wait for the feeling of romance; *do romantic things*. If you do, the feelings will follow.

But even if the feelings don't follow, Scripture would tell you that for now you just have to tough it out and keep doing what God tells you to do. If you don't feel like it or if she doesn't respond—that doesn't matter! You have your marching orders from Heaven itself.

Enter Her World

Another way to love your wife is to enter her world, to show some interest in the things that interest her.

"Frankly, my wife's interests bore me."

Then change your attitude, and get interested anyway.

The Bible instructs men to dwell with their wives "according to knowledge" (1 Peter 3:7 KJV). That means *know* your wife. Know her likes and dislikes. Take time to understand her interests. The passage I quoted above goes on to say that if you don't live like this, your own prayers will be hindered. Did you know that? A man's prayer life can be crippled and rendered ineffective because he is out of alignment with his wife, and he has forgotten that she is supposed to be his best friend.

My wife is my best friend, and I'm not embarrassed to say that. She is my best friend, closest confidant, and most valuable counselor. (She happens to be a very good cook, too.) Even so, Cathe and I are very different people. I don't naturally like a lot of the things that she likes.

For instance, my wife likes to watch cooking shows, often right before we go to sleep. Now this is a problem, because when I watch those shows, I get hungry. She gets ideas, but I get hungry. When we go out to eat, she likes to order soup as an entrée. What? That's like a joke to me. Soup—or salad, for that matter—is *practice*. Soup is just a warm-up before the main event.

Yes, we're very different. But so what? I enter her world, as she enters mine. It's a partnership, walking this road together.

Let me ask husbands a question here. If you were walking down the street with your wife and kids, and a couple of rough-looking characters came toward you in a threatening manner, obviously intending to do harm to your family, what would you do? You'd defend them, of course. You'd deal with those thugs, and do whatever you had to do to shelter the lives of your wife and children.

Or what if your wife and your baby girl were starving, and had no food whatsoever. Would you try to find them some food somewhere?

"Well, of course," you say. "I'm a man."

Okay, but consider this. There are husbands today who have surrendered their roles of spiritual leadership. Their wives and children are being attacked by Satan and his minions while the men stand idly by and do nothing. Their families are starving spiritually, while these men won't lift a finger to help them and see them fed.

Yes, you would defend your wife physically and provide food and shelter for her. Well and good. *But how about doing it spiritually? How about being a man of God and a leader in the home, and realizing that this is your calling.*

You say, "But she isn't submitting to me."

Well, she might if you were doing *your* part.

If we men would truly love our wives as Christ loves the church, they would respond more often as the church responds to Christ.

If you want your wife to blossom, to bloom, to be the woman of God that she can be, *start loving her like Jesus*. Value her. Treasure her. Honor her. Affirm her. Take time for her. And watch what happens. Again, stop worrying about her part—that will take care of itself. You concern yourself with your part.

The problem in many Christian marriages is that we're reading each other's mail, so to speak. The husband quotes verses that apply to his wife, and the wife counters with verses that apply to her husband. The truth is, we should be quoting verses to ourselves about what God has called each of us to do. If you take care of business and stay obedient to the Scriptures, you would be amazed at how your marriage could turn around.

Husbands Are the Initiators

I keep repeating this, but that's okay. In fact, I'll probably repeat it a few more times before I'm done. I firmly believe that it is husbands who hold the key to a flourishing marriage, because they are the initiators. A wife will come into full fruition and submission in response to her husband loving her as he should.

If you think this sounds like a tall order, you're absolutely right. It is. But that is the example we are given to follow. How did Jesus Christ initially demonstrate His love toward us? It was through His death. In John 15:13, Jesus said, "Greater love has no one than this, than to lay down one's life for his friends" (NKJV).

Then in Romans 5:8 we read, "God demonstrates His own love toward us, in that while we were still sinners, Christ died for us" (NKJV).

We were once in rebellion against God, and our hearts were hardened against Him. But one day, we came into a realization of what Jesus did for us. Our hearts softened, and we responded and put our faith in Him. The Bible tells us, "We love Him because He first loved us" (1 John 4:19 NKJV).

So, our love for Christ is a direct response of His persistent and patient love for us. In the same way, a wife's respect of her husband and willingness to follow his leadership is rooted in his loving her as Christ loved the church. Just as the church has responded to Christ because of His overwhelming love, so will a wife respond to her husband for the same reason.

Our goal as husbands should be to simply fulfill God's command to us and leave her reaction up to Him. Why do we love her? So she will submit to us and follow us? No, we love her because we are commanded to.

It is our privilege, and our high calling.

Leading Is Rooted in Paradox

So how do we do that? How do we lead and love like Jesus? Let's look at another passage:

Let nothing be done through selfish ambition or conceit, but in lowliness of mind let each esteem others better than himself. Let each of you look out not only for his own interests, but also for the interests of others.

Let this mind be in you which was also in Christ Jesus, who, being in the form of God, did not consider it robbery to be equal with God, but made Himself of no reputation, taking the form of a bondservant, and coming in the likeness of men. And being found in appearance as a man, He humbled Himself and became obedient to the point of death, even the death of the cross. (Philippians 2:3–8 NKJV)

To love as Christ loves is to place my wife's needs ahead of my own. Remember, Jesus said, "For even the Son of Man did not come to be served, but to serve, and to give His life a ransom for many" (Mark 10:45 NKJV).

He came to serve. And following that example, husbands are to love and serve their wives.

Remember, before a word is given regarding the submission of a wife to her husband, the Bible tells us to submit to one another in the fear of God (see Ephesians 5:21).

Returning to Philippians 2, we read in verse 7 that Jesus "made Himself of no reputation" (NKJV). Another way to translate this is, "He emptied Himself." Did He empty Himself of His divinity? Absolutely not. Never at any time did Jesus cease to be God. He never voided His deity, although you could say that He veiled it. What He did was lay aside the privilege of deity when He walked among us as a man.

Although He was God, although He could do anything He wanted to, He allowed Himself to face the limitations of the human body. He experienced hunger, thirst, weariness, and sorrow. He went through the range of human emotions. He emptied Himself of the privileges of deity, walked among us as a man, and He was our servant. This was so dramatically illustrated in the upper room when Jesus laid aside His outer garment, got down on His hands and knees, and washed the feet of the disciples. Truly, He humbled Himself.

You may be thinking, "I'm not sure I could do that in my home. If I were to humble myself like that, my wife would walk all over me. She would take complete advantage of me."

But that's not necessarily true. And even if it were, so what?

Don't focus so much on her response. Just do what God has called you to do. Don't lecture your wife on what the Bible says to her; take heed of what the Bible says to you as a man and as a husband.

Here is something important to know about leadership: It is rooted in a paradox. The fact is that *true authority comes from humility.*

It's not a matter of weakness, but of meekness. By meekness, I mean power under constraint. Your wife knows what you want to do; she knows what your desire is. But in loving her as Christ loves the church, you must be willing to surrender that.

Dying to Self

So, what does this mean in practical terms for us as husbands?

Well, in my house, for starters, it means letting my wife have the remote control. This is very hard for me, because I'm the original channel-surfer. I'll start clicking that thing when a commercial comes on, because I hate commercials. From there, I'll surf along and watch about three minutes of a program, then go on to something else. I'll watch that for 12 seconds, then something else for 10 minutes. Cathe will just start getting into a program, and then a commercial comes on. Click. I've moved on! It drives her crazy. So, for me to turn that remote control over to her is a pretty good expression of "dying to myself."

For you, dying to yourself and putting your wife's needs above your own might mean something else. I know it's hard to give up that control, but as I said, spiritual authority is rooted in paradox. Jesus said, "But whoever desires to become great among you shall be your servant. And whoever of you desires to be first shall be slave of all" (Mark 10:43–44 NKJV).

In other words, true authority doesn't mean you manipulate your wife or lord it over her. That's not leadership—that's tyranny. In fact, a husband who constantly lectures his wife on his authority probably has very little.

This is not to say that a man shouldn't be firm and decisive and show leadership ability. But it does mean he is to be humble and unselfish. It means he is to rule with humility. It is what God asks of us: "He has shown you, O man, what is good; and what does the LORD require of you but to do justly, to love mercy, and to walk humbly with your God?" (Micah 6:8 NKJV).

Now I know this flies in the face of the stereotypical, macho-man concept of the tough guy who asserts himself, is always in control, and whose wife comes at his beck and call.

But that is not God's way.

Nor is it loving our wives as God has called us to. The fact is, it takes more courage, strength, and discipline for a man to humble himself than to assert himself. What it takes is true love. And God requires nothing less.

Helping or Hindering?

Ephesians 5 goes on to say: "Husbands, love your wives, just as Christ also loved the church and gave Himself for her, that He might sanctify and cleanse her with the washing of water by the word" (verses 25–26 NKJV).

No one can be a greater hindrance to a wife's spiritual growth than her husband. But by the same token, no one can be a greater encouragement. A husband's first priority is to make sure his wife is properly aligned with God. He recognizes that her personal happiness as a woman, a wife, and a mother all hinge on that.

Some husbands might say, "That's her problem, not mine."

No, it is *your* problem.

Why? Because God has called us husbands to be the spiritual leaders in our homes, and to treat our wives with honor and care.

As we've already seen, the apostle Peter tells us, "You husbands must be careful of your wives, being thoughtful of their needs and honoring them as the weaker sex. Remember that you and your wife are partners in receiving God's blessings, and if you don't treat her as you should, your prayers will not get ready answers" (1 Peter 3:7 TLB).

This is the same principle Jesus was speaking of when He said, "Therefore if you bring your gift to the altar, and there remember that your brother has something against you, leave your gift there before the altar, and go your way. First be reconciled to your brother, and then come and offer your gift" (Matthew 5:23–24 NKJV).

We must take care of our home and lead. Our priorities should be:

God first

Family second

Occupation third

I know this is hard to do. It isn't any easier for me than it is for any other man. I have to consistently ask myself, am I loving my wife as Christ loves the church? Am I laying my life down? Am I being the leader God has called me to be? It's actually a constant process of realignment and fine-tuning, because we can be doing great as husbands and fathers one day, and fall short the next.

It Comes from Him

You may be thinking, "I have to take the spiritual lead, and the primary responsibility for my marriage and home rests on my shoulders. But that seems overwhelming to me! How can I do that? How can I pull it off? I can't."

Quite honestly, I can't pull this off either, because these things don't come naturally for me. I'm not naturally wired to be humble, unselfish, and focused on the needs of others. No one is.

So, what do we do? In an earlier chapter we talked about the importance of being filled with the Spirit. We need Him so much! We absolutely can't accomplish these things on our own. We need supernatural help. This love that God commands for us to have for our wives has to come from Him, or it will never come at all.

I've been encouraged a number of times by the words of Romans 5:5, where Paul writes: "Now hope does not disappoint, because the love of God has been poured out in our hearts by the Holy Spirit who was given to us" (NKJV).

I don't have to squeeze *agape* love out of my heart like I'd squeeze juice out of an orange. Actually, I could squeeze forever and never get a drop. If I have God's love in my heart at all, it's because He is in the process of pouring it into me. And as He pours it in, I have the privilege of pouring it out. It will come as a result of walking closely with Him, because "the fruit of the Spirit is love" (Galatians 5:22 NKJV).

You won't get there overnight. It will take a lifetime. But determine to move in that direction today and say, "I will be the man God has called me to be. From this day forward, I will seek to love my wife as Christ loved the church."

Prayer: Lord, at the very heart of agape love is the truth that "we love because You first loved us." Thank You, Father, for loving us so much that You sent Your only Son to die for us. Please remind us of this often. We get so wrapped up in superficial things that we forget our marriage is only as strong as our love for You and each other. Lead us in each of our roles as You created them. Most of all, lead us in Your great love. In Jesus' name, amen.

QUESTIONS for Discussion

1. "Every marriage will face difficulties and challenges. . . . In fact, sometimes this is what makes a good marriage." Do you agree with this statement? In what ways can hardships or tough times actually strengthen a marriage? Why do crises bond some husbands and wives even closer together, while other marriages fall apart under such pressure? What makes the difference?

2. It seems natural for a husband to expect his wife to "do her part" as outlined in Scripture. Why then does Greg say that husbands need to banish that question from their minds?

3.   Do you think it is overstated when it is said that the ultimate responsibility for the success of a marriage rests directly on the man's shoulders? Why or why not?

4.   Greg says one of the biggest problems men have—even Christian men—is falling into a pattern of passivity. Why does he assert that if men continue in that pattern, they will drag others down with them?

5.   There was an important statement mentioned regarding men's leadership: "When husbands refuse to lead, they put their wives in positions they were never meant to fulfill." What specific roles have women felt pressured to fill? Since God truly expects a husband to be the spiritual leader in his home, how does his apathy and passivity affect everyone under his roof—and beyond?

6.   "Husbands, love your wives" (Ephesians 5:25 NKJV). Since *agape* is the Greek word for "love" in this verse *and* in John 3:16, what does that tell us about the nature, character, and depth of that love?

7.   This chapter said, "If a loving husband is willing to sacrifice his own life for his wife, then how much more should he be willing to make lesser sacrifices for her—such as his own likes and dislikes, desires, opinions, preferences, and personal welfare?" Is this statement a reasonable description of what the *agape* love of a husband for his wife ought to look like in a marriage, or does it go too far? What specific areas of daily life ought to be impacted by this determination?

8.   In a further description of a husband's *agape* love for his wife, it is stated: "It's not just being 'pleasant' or 'nice' (though that's a good place to start). It is rather a deep affection and involvement, even if the object of that love seems unlovable at times." What would a man's natural response be to a wife who has somehow become "unlovable"? What does this tell us about our huge need for a supernatural ability to love as God calls us to love?

9.   This chapter encourages men to "do what [they] did for [their wives] in the early days of [their] relationship." Set about winning her love and affection all over again. Don't wait for some random surge of

emotion to get started—just do it." What kinds of behavior, conversation, planning, and thoughtfulness characterize the "early days" of a romance? What could a husband do to begin winning the heart of his wife all over again? As Greg writes: "Don't wait for the feeling of romance; do romantic things. If you do, the feelings will follow."

10. Husbands, how can you begin to enter your wife's world (even a little bit) as you practice the selfless *agape* love that is sourced in God?

CHAPTER 6

Standing Strong Against Temptation

"God blesses the people who patiently endure testing and temptation. Afterward they will receive the crown of life that God has promised to those who love him."
—James 1:12 (NLT)

Jonathan's Story: When I lost my brother in 2008, I woke up multiple times per night over the following weeks, months, and even years. I would wake up feeling like there was a chest wound that had just opened up. I grieved so deeply, my pillow would be covered in tears. I was devastated. I still miss him desperately, and I look forward to seeing him again one day.

But at the time my brother went to be with the Lord, I was a drug user, and nothing was more appealing to me than to smoke some weed, drink some alcohol, take some pills, or rely on some chemical to take the edge off. Marijuana, in particular was big draw for me at the time. And more than ever, people are using substances to escape.

My ultimate point is, whatever you're using to escape or endure, God is so much more powerful. He is so much more powerful than you could ever think or imagine. Don't rob yourself of the opportunity to depend on God.

When I was not walking with Him, I abused those things to feel good. And yeah, you might feel "good" for a minute. You might feel high or happy, but it's a false, momentary "happiness." But listen, here's the truth: Pain was the catalyst that brought me closer to God. Pain was the catalyst that made me look to His promises, that made me look to a hope that was beyond this life, a hope beyond the grave.

It was faith in Jesus Christ that rescued me. God was there for me. The church was there for me. And His Word did bring comfort. Yes, there were tears and pain, but I did not grieve as those who had no hope. This is an area where we must be sober-minded. We are spiritual beings, and the Bible warns us clearly not to be brought under the power of anything.

As Paul said in 1 Corinthians 6:12, "All things are lawful for me, but all things are not helpful. All things are lawful for me, but I will not be brought under the power of any" (NKJV).

We live in a culture today that is obsessed with sex: before marriage, outside of marriage, and in almost every perverse form imaginable. It just seems to get worse all the time. If historians were to look back at our time—at our movies, TV shows, magazines, and billboards—they would certainly have to conclude that this was a sex-obsessed culture.

Of course, none of this should surprise us.

Jesus Himself said that the last days would be filled with wickedness comparable to the days of Noah and the days of Lot:

> When I return the world will be as indifferent to the things of God as the people were in Noah's day. They ate and drank and married—everything just as usual right up to the day when Noah went into the ark and the Flood came and destroyed them all.
>
> And the world will be as it was in the days of Lot: people went about their daily business—eating and drinking, buying and sell-

ing, farming and building—until the morning Lot left Sodom. Then fire and brimstone rained down from heaven and destroyed them all. Yes, it will be "business as usual" right up to the hour of my return. (Luke 17:26–30 TLB)

Both of those eras in human history were characterized by unbridled sexual perversion. Of course, all of these things undermine marriages and families. Adultery has spread throughout our society, and we see its effects all around. But how widespread is it? According to some statistics, more than 60 percent of all men have had extramarital affairs,[11] and nearly 70 percent of all married men under 40 expect to have an extramarital relationship.[12] But if you think this problem is unique to men, think again. Women are catching up. Unfaithfulness on the part of women toward their husbands is now almost equal with that of the men.

Are you committing adultery? Are you planning to? Have you been thinking about it? Considering the statistics, it's entirely possible. I just want you to think for a few moments about the repercussions and the damage this sin can bring to you, your spouse, and your family. So significant is the sin of adultery that it made the top ten—the Ten Commandments, that is. God says, "You shall not commit adultery" (Exodus 20:14 NKJV). Then He expands on it: "You shall not covet your neighbor's wife" (verse 17).

Why did God give us commandments like these? It was for our own protection, because He knows what devastation it can bring.

The Bible asks, "Can a man take fire to his bosom, and his clothes not be burned?" (Proverbs 6:27 NKJV). The answer, of course, is no. If you scoop red-hot coals onto your chest, you'll soon understand the consequences. A fire can get out of control so easily. And so can lust! You think, "I can contain this. I can handle this. This is no problem." Then suddenly the burning embers of lust are blowing over your life, and you've lost all control.

What happened? You took fire into your bosom, or into your heart or into your life, and you were burned. You were one of the many who thought they could handle it.

That's what Samson deluded himself into thinking. He must have thought, "What is this lady Delilah going to do to me? I'm the mighty Samson. I can tear apart a young lion with my bare hands. I can kill a thousand Philistines with the jawbone of a donkey. What impact can one little woman have on me?"

But the devil was sly. He knew he could never bring Samson down on the battlefield, so he brought him down in the bedroom. It was a sneak attack through this woman Delilah, whose name, ironically, means "delicate." She began to break down Samson's resolve and resistance until he finally confessed to her the secret of his supernatural strength (see Judges 16:16–21). If only he could have come to his senses and realized he was falling into a trap.

It's the same thing with lust. It's devastating, and it destroys thousands of marriages today, as well as ruins the lives of countless young people. Aside from the moral and emotional implications, it's also killing people and ravaging lives through sexually transmitted diseases.

Thinking Naively

You might be thinking, "Did you have to devote an entire chapter to temptation, especially sexual sin? I really don't need to hear this. I would never fall into this sin. My spouse and I have an ideal marriage. I can't imagine any circumstances in which I would ever be unfaithful."

I remember listening to an interview with a man who had written some Christian books on the family. This man had boasted to his friends, "If I ever fall into sin, I guarantee it will not be adultery. Anything but. I love my wife so much that it would never happen to me."

Do you know what happened? You guessed it. This man fell into the sin of adultery, and ended up doing the very things he said he would never, ever do. He concluded the interview with these highly significant words: "An unguarded strength is a double weakness."

How true! Whenever we say things like, "I would never fall into that sin," we're already on very thin ice. It's almost like issuing a challenge to Satan and his demons to attack us in a given area of our lives.

And that would be very, very foolish.

In 1 Corinthians 10:12, we read: "So let the man who feels sure of his standing today be careful that he does not fall tomorrow" (PHI).

The Message Bible paraphrases the verse like this: "Don't be so naive and self-confident. You're not exempt. You could fall flat on your face as easily as anyone else. Forget about self-confidence; it's useless. Cultivate God-confidence."

Any of us are capable of committing any sin. Don't ever forget that.

You are capable of doing terrible, unthinkable things, and so am I. As the prophet Jeremiah warns us: "The heart is deceitful above all things, and desperately wicked" (Jeremiah 17:9 NKJV).

Over in the New Testament, the apostle Paul declares: "I know I am rotten through and through so far as my old sinful nature is concerned. No matter which way I turn I can't make myself do right. I want to but I can't. When I want to do good, I don't; and when I try not to do wrong, I do it anyway" (Romans 7:18–19 TLB).

That doesn't mean I will actually do all these sinful things, but it certainly means the *potential* is always there. We dare not let down our guard.

Peter warned his listeners: "Be sober [well balanced and self-disciplined], be alert and cautious at all times. That enemy of yours, the devil, prowls around like a roaring lion [fiercely hungry], seeking someone to devour" (1 Peter 5:8 AMP).

If I allow temptation to infiltrate my life and my old nature to prevail, I could fall, just as surely as a fire will spread if gasoline is poured on it. But if I take practical steps and precautions to guard myself and to stay close to the Lord, then I don't have to fall.

Withstanding the Culture (Daniel's Strength)

If you remember the story of Daniel, the young Israelite living in captivity in a foreign nation, he was the prime example of standing strong against temptation. Though he was young, and could have "lived it up" in Babylon, he determined, "I'm not going to eat the food of the Babylonians. I'm not going to worship in the way of the Babylonians. I'm going to stand true to God and His commands."

Daniel lived completely contrary to the culture. And this is what we need to do today. We need young men and young women who will say, "I am going to stand like Daniel." I am not going to fall to the pressures of society. I'm not going to cave to what everybody else is doing because that's what's easy. No, my identity is in Christ. He has a plan for my life. He has a purpose for my marriage. We need more young people to do this, and we need more old people to do this as well. We all need to follow Daniel's example.

Rejecting the Invitation (Balaam's Error)

In warning believers about fornication, Paul said, "Nor let us commit sexual immorality, as some of them did, and in one day twenty-three thousand fell" (1 Corinthians 10:8 NKJV).

Paul refers here to the book of Numbers and the story of the greedy prophet Balaam, who was a sort of "prophet for hire."

When Balak, the king of the Moabites, wanted the Israelites defeated, he thought that finding a prophet to curse them and bring God's judgment on them would be much easier than having to defeat them on the battlefield.

I don't know where he found a prophet like Balaam. Maybe he looked in the Moab Yellow Pages under "profit" because that seems to be all Balaam was interested in. Whatever the case, he secured Balaam's services, told him to go and curse Israel, and offered a very generous contract to do it. No problem, Balaam said. So, he went out to curse Israel, but God spoke to Balaam and told him not to curse Israel, but to bless them.

This didn't exactly endear him to Balak. He hadn't hired a top-gun prophet to bless the people; he hired him to curse them. Still, Balaam was determined to somehow find a way to get this money. He went on his way to do what God had told him not to do, and in one of the Bible's most attention-grabbing narratives, his donkey spoke to him. You would think that would have been enough for Balaam right then and there. But he persisted and eventually devised a plan.

"I'll tell you what, Balak," the reckless prophet most likely counseled. "I can't curse the Israelites. God has told me not to. But I have an idea. If you can get some of your young, sensual Moabite women to entice these young Israelite men to go into their tents and have sexual relations with them, that is a way you can get them to worship the false gods. If these Israelite men actually enter the tents and engage in this idolatry, this will bring God's wrath on the people, and He will judge them."

"Good idea," Balak probably said, and he enlisted the women to do the work. So, the young women went out, and it was a success—depending on how you look at it. The story is recorded in Numbers 25, where we read,

> Now Israel remained in Acacia Grove, and the people began to commit harlotry with the women of Moab. They invited the people to the sacrifices of their gods, and the people ate and bowed down to their gods. So Israel was joined to Baal of Peor, and the anger of the LORD was aroused against Israel. Then the LORD said to Moses, "Take all the leaders of the people and hang the offenders before the LORD, out in the sun, that the fierce anger of the LORD may turn away from Israel." (verses 1–4 NKJV)

These weren't the first people to be destroyed by immorality, and they won't be the last. Paul emphasized this to the church of Corinth, and to believers living in the last days. You see, the Corinthian believers were a bit smug. They somehow thought they would never fall into sexual sin or idolatry. This is why Paul framed these words in the way he did.

Ironically, immorality was rampant in Corinth in Paul's day. In fact, towering above the ruins of old Corinth is a 2,000-foot mountain fortress called Acrocorinth. Situated at the top of that mountain was the Temple of Aphrodite, the Greek goddess of fertility, and as many as a thousand priestesses, or prostitutes, working for the temple, carried on their immoral activities in worship of this pagan deity.

It is said that the prostitutes from this temple would go into the city of Corinth wearing specially designed sandals that left the words "follow me" imprinted on the sand.[13]

Many citizens of Corinth did just that. They followed the prostitutes to the temple and committed sexual immorality as well as idolatry. I think the same invitation to commit sexual immorality is being extended to us today by way of the media's constant bombardment of our culture with sex. The message is hard to miss: "Follow me."

Watching Your Step (David's Defeat)

Usually, the steps that lead to sexual immorality, including adultery, are numerous. It happens over a period of time, generally beginning in the area of the imagination, and then leading up to the act itself.

We see this in the life of one man who committed adultery and paid the price for it in the years to come. His name was David. Sadly, when you think of David's life, two names come up that sum up his whole story—David and Goliath, and David and Bathsheba. One represents his greatest triumph, while the other represents his greatest defeat.

I've referenced David and Bathsheba a couple of times already, but I'd like to highlight an additional point or two. The incident began in the spring, when the Bible tells us that kings were going out to battle. All of the kings, except David, who was taking some time off. He was out strolling on his patio when he looked down and saw a beautiful woman named Bathsheba bathing herself. Now, he couldn't have avoided that first look—and sometimes you wonder if Bathsheba allowed herself to be in a place where she would be seen by David, knowing she was within view.

Maybe or maybe not. One thing we do know is that the Bible never points the finger at her. David was the culprit in this case. He couldn't have avoided that first look, but the second one is probably what got him into trouble. He then began to devise a plan in which he could have Bathsheba. Misusing his authority and position as king, he commanded her to be brought up to his chambers. He had sexual relations with her, and she became pregnant. But instead of confessing his sin to God, he tried to cover up what he had done. So, he sent word that Bathsheba's husband, Uriah, who was serving David in his army, was to be brought back to be with his wife. David wanted to cover it up.

Uriah was brought back, but David hadn't reckoned on the fact of this brave soldier's rock-solid integrity. How could Uriah have the pleasure of being with his wife when his fellow soldiers were out risking their lives on the battlefield? In spite of what the king said, Uriah determined to sleep outside his own house that night.

David should have stopped right there.

I think it was a moment of grace, a moment where he might have caught himself and saved himself from falling into still deeper sin. It was as though God was putting an obstacle in his path, trying to warn him. But David persisted. He got Uriah drunk, then sent him in to be with his wife. Again, Uriah would not have relations with his wife.

So, David ordered his commander to have Uriah sent to the front lines, where he was killed in the heat of battle. Then, without wasting much time, David took Bathsheba into his home and married her. David may have thought he pulled it off, but it doesn't work that way. The Bible says, "He who covers his sins will not prosper" (Proverbs 28:13 NKJV).

For 12 terrible months, David lived out of harmony and fellowship with the God he loved so much. He later wrote in the psalms about what it's like to live out of fellowship with God when there is unconfessed sin, and his words still ring so true to any who have ever been in a similar position.

Take a few moments and ponder David's anguished words:

> When I kept it all inside,
>
> my bones turned to powder,
>
> my words became daylong groans.
>
> The pressure never let up;
>
> all the juices of my life dried up. (Psalm 32:3–4 MSG)

If you are engaged in unconfessed sin right now, be it in action or even in the realm of the imagination, then you know what David is talking about. You know the destruction that that sin can bring. That is why the Bible tells us in Proverbs 6:32, "But the man who commits adultery is an utter fool, for he destroys himself" (NLT).

If you choose to commit adultery, then you are choosing self-destruction.

Building Walls of Protection

You might remember the story of Nehemiah in the Old Testament. He was the guy who helped rebuild the walls of Jerusalem in just 52 days. Now, that is some serious efficiency! But here's what's even more amazing. The leaders of Israel stepped forward, not just to celebrate the success of the rebuilding of the walls, but to confess their failures, repent, and commit to something greater. Their example led the nation to renewal, restoring their relationship with God and laying a foundation for a future built on his truth.

So, how does this relate to our topic? It shows what is possible. It encourages us to take the steps needed to stand strong against temptation, and to prevent the devastating sin of sexual immorality. It tells us there are things we can do to build a wall of protection around our lives and around our marriages.

1. Walk with God

This point is simple, but true. If a husband or wife is truly walking with God, it will give him or her the power to stand strong against temptation and say, like Joseph, "How then can I do this great wickedness, and sin against God?" (Genesis 39:9 NKJV).

It was David's failure to do this that made him vulnerable to the temptations he faced. You'd think that David, "the man after God's own heart," would have stopped himself after looking at Bathsheba, and said, "What am I thinking? How could I do such a thing? How could I sin against the God who loves me and has cared for me through all of these years?" But David evidently hadn't been walking with God for some time, because when the temptation came, it seems he didn't give the Lord a second thought.

It was Job who said, "I have made a covenant with my eyes; why then should I look upon a young woman?" (Job 31:1 NKJV). In effect, he said, "I am guarding myself. I am careful as to what I look at."

On the same subject, Jesus said,

> You have heard that it was said to those of old, "You shall not commit adultery." But I say to you that whoever looks at a woman to lust for her has already committed adultery with her in his heart. If your right eye causes you to sin, pluck it out and cast it from you; for it is more profitable for you that one of your members perish, than for your whole body to be cast into hell. (Matthew 5:27–29 NKJV)

When Jesus used the phrase "looks at a woman," He wasn't just talking about just seeing her. Nor was He talking about being exposed to something you didn't want to be exposed to. The fact is, we can't always control our environment and what's thrown in front of us—particularly in our sex-saturated media world. But again, Jesus wasn't speaking about a casual glance here. What He referred to was a deliberate, continual act of looking. In this usage, the idea is not of an incidental or involuntarily glance, but an intentional and repeated gazing with the express purpose of lusting. I might also add that this statement doesn't apply to men only. It also applies to women looking lustfully at men.

So, what this refers to here is a person who actually goes out of his or her way to look at someone in order to lust after them. This could happen in real life, and it could also happen via the internet, where a person deliberately downloads provocative, lustful images to stare at.

And here is Jesus' solution: "If your right eye causes you to sin, pluck it out and cast it from you" (Matthew 5:29 NKJV).

You say, "Isn't that a little radical?" Yes, but it's not literal. If we took this literally, there wouldn't be many people left with a right eye. Obviously, Jesus wasn't speaking literally, because if you pluck out your right eye, you could still lust with your left. So, we need to understand the culture of the time, which is often helpful in interpreting various passages of Scripture.

In Jewish culture, the right hand represented a person's best and most precious faculties, and the right eye represented one's best vision. What Jesus was saying, in essence, is that you should be willing to give up whatever is necessary to keep from falling into sin. Whatever steps you have to take that would prevent you from falling morally or spiritually, take them. If there is something in your life, whether it's a relationship or something you're doing that causes you to commit this sin of looking with lust, then you need to stop. Now. Looking always leads to doing. If it isn't stopped at some point, then sooner or later, you'll be tired of just looking and want to start doing. That's why it needs to be nipped in the bud—in the realm of your mind.

The Bible says, "Walk in the Spirit, and you shall not fulfill the lust of the flesh" (Galatians 5:16 NKJV). The best defense is a good offense. So, walk with God.

2. Walk with your spouse

Walking in oneness with your spouse includes a close and intimate friendship, as well as a romantic connection. Friendship and companionship between couples is at the very foundation of a marriage. We talked about this earlier in the book, but I can't emphasize it enough. Your spouse should be your best friend.

Building on that warm and affectionate friendship, keep the romance alive in your marriage. Cultivate it. If the romance is dying, then get it back and throw some more logs on the fire. Do what you can to rekindle it again.

Take care to sexually fulfill one other. The Bible tells you, "Drink water from your own cistern, and running water from your own well" (Proverbs 5:15 NKJV).

Find fulfillment in your marriage relationship as husband and wife, as God has created you and has blessed that union. Guard this intimate area of your love relationship, and don't let anything keep you from fulfilling one another's desires.

3. Walk as an example to your children

We might not want to believe this, especially if we're not particularly proud of the decisions we've made, but our children will walk in our footsteps. Our children, grandchildren, and great-grandchildren will likely choose the path set before them. And so, husbands, wives, fathers, mothers, grandmothers, and grandfathers, take heed in the way you walk, lest you stumble.

As John said in 3 John 4, "I have no greater joy than to hear that my children are walking in the truth" (ESV).

If we want our children to walk in truth, we have to model it for them. Our actions today lay the foundation that our children and our descendants will build their lives upon. That is the ultimate warning today. For better or worse, the choices we make today matter for generations to come.

Galatians 6:7 reminds us, "Whatever a man sows, that he will also reap" (NKJV).

Whether you sow to the flesh or you sow to the Spirit, you are going to reap the consequences. If you sow to the Spirit, following God and walking close in your relationship with Him, you're going to be blessed. Your wife's going to be blessed, your husband's going to be blessed, your career is going to be blessed, and your children are going to be blessed.

4. Do not walk in the counsel of the ungodly

At all costs, avoid any relationship or friendship that could cause you to fall.

If you find yourself in a questionable relationship with someone of the opposite sex right now, if you're flirting and playing around, then it's time to push on the brakes. "Oh, it's innocent," you might say. But please listen—you never know what it could lead to. Avoid this danger at all costs. Scripture tells us to avoid even the appearance of evil (see 1 Thessalonians 5:22 KJV).

Count the cost. Remember some of the warnings we've been looking at. These strong cautions, along with an intense love for God and your spouse, can see you through the rough waters of sexual temptation.

Temptation will be around as long as we live. But we don't have to fall into it if we take the steps God has given us. And if you have fallen into it, *stop*. Repent. Turn around. Don't take one more step in the wrong direction. Thank God there is forgiveness, and learn from your mistakes.

Let's not forget the words of 1 Corinthians 10:13, "No temptation has overtaken you except such as is common to man; but God is faithful, who will not allow you to be tempted beyond what you are able, but with the temptation will also make the way of escape, that you may be able to bear it."

This clearly tells us that God won't give us more than we can handle. He won't let us be tempted above our capacity to resist. So, you don't have to give in to that impure thought. You don't have to give in to that sinful idea. You don't have to visit those questionable sites on the Internet.

You can't stop yourself from being tempted, but remember this: The tempter needs the cooperation of the temptee! We are tempted, the Bible says, when we are drawn away by our own lusts and enticed (see James 1:14). So, while it's true that temptation can be strong, it won't overpower you if you refuse to cooperate with it.

As has been said, you can't stop a bird from flying over your head, but you can stop it from building a nest in your hair. It's not a sin to be tempted. Jesus was tempted, after all. But it is a sin to give in to temptation.

Don't forget that God is always ready to help you in this struggle against your old nature. Psalm 46:1 reminds us that "God is our refuge and strength, a very present help in trouble" (NKJV). In the Lord's Prayer, Jesus leads us to pray, "And do not lead us into temptation, but deliver us from the evil one" (NKJV). He wouldn't have given us that prayer if He didn't mean for us to use it. Seek God's face and pray to be delivered from the presence and power of Satan's lures, traps, and schemes.

In the Garden of Gethsemane, Jesus said to His men, "Watch and pray so that you will not fall into temptation. The spirit is willing, but the flesh is weak" (Matthew 26:41 NIV). That's still wonderful counsel for you and me every day of our lives.

The fact is, when it comes to devastating sexual sin, you *do* have a choice in the matter. As Moses once said to the people of Israel, "Choose life" (Deuteronomy 30:19 NKJV).

Prayer: Lord, please help us choose life by following You. We want to walk in Your footsteps. We want to follow Your commands. We want to avoid temptation and uphold our marriage covenant. Thank You for being our comfort in times of grief. Thank You for giving us spouses to love and cherish.

Whether we grew up in a loving, flourishing Christian home that taught us the essentials of the faith, or whether we grew up in a dysfunctional home, what matters most is the decision we make when it comes to our relationship with You. You have given us life and life more abundantly; You have given us your Holy Spirit. Help us walk in newness of life as Your children, overcoming every temptation with Your strength. In Jesus' name, amen.

QUESTIONS for Discussion

1. Jonathan shares how "more than ever, people are using substances to escape." How does temptation lure you to escape your troubles, looking to other things for false comfort? How does 1 Corinthians 6:12 remind you not to fall under the power of anything other than the Holy Spirit? "All things are lawful for me, but all things are not helpful. All things are lawful for me, but I will not be brought under the power of any" (NKJV).

2. Read Proverbs 6:27–29. What does this passage say to an individual who says about lust, "I can handle it. I can play with it just a little without doing much harm"?

3. Discuss the danger of considering a sin like adultery and saying to yourself, "It could never happen to me. I could never do anything like that".

4. A man who had sworn it "could never happen to me" fell into adultery after all. Later, the man wrote: "An unguarded strength is a double weakness." What does that statement mean to you?

5. *The Message* Bible paraphrases 1 Corinthians 10:12 with these words: "Don't be so naive and self-confident. You're not exempt. You could fall flat on your face as easily as anyone else. Forget about self-confidence; it's useless. Cultivate God-confidence." Forget self-confidence? That certainly goes against the grain of our culture, doesn't it? Contrast self-confidence with God-confidence. Why do we need God-confidence to stand against temptation and sin?

6. The apostle Peter writes: "Be alert and of sober mind. Your enemy the devil prowls around like a roaring lion looking for someone to devour. Resist him, standing firm in the faith, because you know that the family of believers throughout the world is undergoing the same kind of sufferings" (1 Peter 5:8–9 NIV). What practical steps can we take to make sure we walk through our day "alert" and ready to resist Satan's attacks?

7. Read Psalm 32:1–5. What did David experience when he tried to cover over his sins, rather than dealing with them before God? What was the result when he finally decided to open up his life for God's inspection and cleansing?

8. How would daily praying David's prayer in Psalm 139:23–24 keep us from falling into destructive sins?

9. Read Matthew 5:27–29. Why does Jesus use such a drastic word picture here? What is He saying about those things/places/people/habits in our lives that continually trip us up and lead us into sin?

10. The Bible says, "Walk in the Spirit, and you shall not fulfill the lust of the flesh" (Galatians 5:16 NKJV). There's an old football expression that says, "The best defense is a good offense." How would you apply that saying to walking with God and seeking to avoid sin?

11. This chapter said, "Our actions today lay the foundation that our children and our descendants will build their lives upon." How does this warn us of the ripple effect our sins have on the next generation? How can we model truth to our children, so they also walk in truth?

12. Meditate on Moses' powerful words to the Israelites: "Choose life" (Deuteronomy 30:19 NKJV). How is standing strong against temptation choosing life?

CHAPTER 7

The Incredible Power of Words

*"Words kill, words give life;
They're either poison or fruit—you choose."*
—Proverbs 18:21 (MSG)

A few years ago, Cathe and I were invited to stay at a cabin in Virginia that belonged to some friends. This cabin didn't have any heat to speak of, except for a fireplace and a little furnace downstairs that had to be fed a regular diet of logs.

"I know this might sound stupid," I told the owners, "but I don't know how to build a fire very well."

"Well," they said, "the first thing you have to do is go out and get some kindling."

"Okay. Where do you buy that?"

"You don't buy it," they told me. "You go find it. Kindling is the little sticks and branches that you use to start the fire."

"Oh."

Then they showed me the proper way to start a fire, and pointed out that once the fireplace was filled with enough ash, I would need to scoop it out, put it into a metal bucket, and then keep the bucket on a concrete surface so all of the embers would cool down.

"Be careful to make sure they've all cooled down," they cautioned. "They do stay quite live for a period of time."

It was freezing cold outside, and since our California blood is so thin, we had to keep the fireplace and furnace going nonstop. I would get up at 3:00 AM to add more wood to the fires. After a while, however, the fireplace was filled with ashes. I got out the shovel and filled the bucket all the way to the brim. After waiting for what I thought had been a couple of days, I decided it was time to empty the bucket. It was late at night, and Cathe was already asleep. I went outside in my pj's and slippers, took the bucket of ash, and pitched the ash out into the forest.

Looking back now, it was one of those moments where it seemed like everything was moving in slow motion. Much to my horror, I saw, in the ash, these little burning embers. Immediately, small fires were starting— three fires right off the bat. I started picking up the live, burning embers with my hands and throwing them up on the driveway.

Then a breeze came along, and more little fires erupted. I ran into the cabin to look for some kind of bucket and found one that looked slightly larger than a drinking glass. Quickly filling it with water, I poured it on one of my fires, and ran back again for more water.

You'd better believe that I was calling on the Lord for help. I thought I would burn the whole forest down—and Cathe and myself with it—but fortunately, that didn't happen. The rest of the night, however, I kept looking out through the window, thinking I would see a huge forest fire erupt at any moment.

That experience reminded me of the truth of the statement James made when he said, "So also, the tongue is a small thing, but what enormous damage it can do. A great forest can be set on fire by one tiny spark" (James 3:5 TLB).

How true that is. More people have died by the power of the tongue than by any other weapon humanity has ever devised.

The World's Most Dangerous Weapon

Today, manufacturers put warning labels on their products, so we won't do something stupid. They're trying to protect themselves from potential lawsuits. Consider all of the safety standards we have in place for everything from automobile emissions to gun control. Yet the most dangerous weapon and the most toxic pollutant is left unchecked: the tongue.

We desperately need to learn how to control it, and especially in our marriages. If we were brutally honest, I'm sure we could look back on this past year (or maybe even the past week) and admit we have said a few things to our spouse that we've lived to regret.

Dedicated to God, our tongues can be a powerful force for good in our marriages and in the lives of those around us. But left unchecked, especially when yielded to the enemy, the tongue is the most destructive weapon on the face of the earth. It has the terrible potential to tear down marriages and destroy lives.

As followers of Jesus Christ, we know a lot about certain sins we should avoid. We know that we aren't supposed to lie. We know that we aren't supposed to steal. We know that we aren't supposed to be immoral. We go out of our way to avoid things that would drag us down spiritually.

Yet one thing we are warned about many times in Scripture is often left unchecked among believers. It is also an area that is grossly neglected by many husbands and wives . . . and that is *thinking about what we say.*

For example, we would never dream of taking out a knife and thrusting it into our husband or wife. Yet we can wound our partner deeply with a few carelessly spoken words. These are spiritual wounds, and they can leave scars that last every bit as long as physical wounds.

Most of us can remember hurtful words and taunts from the earliest days of childhood. Years and decades may roll by, but simply recalling those harsh or degrading words has the power to bring pain to the soul.

The book of James offers some wise observations about the tongue:

> We all stumble in many ways. Anyone who is never at fault in what they say is perfect, able to keep their whole body in check.
>
> When we put bits into the mouths of horses to make them obey us, we can turn the whole animal. Or take ships as an example.

Although they are so large and are driven by strong winds, they are steered by a very small rudder wherever the pilot wants to go. Likewise, the tongue is a small part of the body, but it makes great boasts. Consider what a great forest is set on fire by a small spark. The tongue also is a fire, a world of evil among the parts of the body. It corrupts the whole body, sets the whole course of one's life on fire, and is itself set on fire by hell.

All kinds of animals, birds, reptiles and sea creatures are being tamed and have been tamed by mankind, but no human being can tame the tongue. It is a restless evil, full of deadly poison.

With the tongue we praise our Lord and Father, and with it we curse human beings, who have been made in God's likeness. Out of the same mouth come praise and cursing. My brothers, this should not be. (James 3:2–10 NIV)

James tells us that the tongue is like a fire, like a bit, like a beast, and like a poison, among other things. Take James' example of the bit. We can make a large, powerful horse turn around almost midstride and go wherever we want by means of a small bit in its mouth. A few years ago, at the Rose Parade, I watched a man riding a buffalo down the street. He had a saddle on it and a bit in its mouth. It was amazing to me that this rider could control a massive beast with a tiny bit. Just as a bit controls a horse (or a buffalo, in some cases), we are controlled by our words.

One word can virtually set the course that your life takes. Saying "I do" to a partner in marriage means a lifetime of commitment. Saying "I won't" to the temptation of an extramarital affair could save that marriage from destruction. Of course, saying "I will" to Jesus Christ will forever change your eternal destiny.

Our tongues control us. What we say affects what we do. It also profoundly affects our marriages.

The tongue is a small thing, but what an enormous amount of damage it can do. The mere 2 ounces of mucous membrane in our mouths can do so much evil or so much good. Think of those who have dedicated their words to darkness and to the devil. There was Adolf Hitler, for example, who, through his demonic rhetoric, led an entire nation down the pathway to Hell, and caused the useless and needless slaughter of countless people. This is what a tongue dedicated to the devil can do.

Then we have the example of someone who dedicated his words to God: Billy Graham. The result was millions of people who gave their lives to Jesus Christ. So, to whom—and to what—are you dedicating your words? Are you dedicating them to God, and toward the goal of building up your husband, your wife, your family, and other people God has placed in your life?

Quick to Listen

James 1:19 is a verse I think we should post where we can see it on a daily basis: "My dear brothers and sisters, take note of this: Everyone should be quick to listen, slow to speak and slow to become angry" (NIV).

The problem is that too often we are swift to speak, slow to listen, and quick to get angry!

What does it mean to be "quick to listen"?

I think it implies taking time to hear someone out. Have you ever made a statement to your spouse or your children based on an incorrect understanding of what was happening, because you didn't take the time to hear them out? You were quick to make a snap judgment, and just as quick to sound off about it. That's why the Bible says, "He who answers a matter before he hears it, it is folly and shame to him" (Proverbs 18:13 NKJV).

In our era of instant messaging and 10-second sound bites, we find it difficult to slow down, be still, and truly *listen*. But the Bible says we need to be quick about that. We need to be quick to listen and especially quick to hear what our husband or wife has to say.

Failure to Communicate

One of the more famous Hollywood lines emerged from the Paul Newman movie *Cool Hand Luke*. Just after hitting the escaped prisoner Luke with a baton, sending him sprawling, the prison guard drawls, "What we got here ... is a failure to communicate."

Most communication breakdowns will never be as extreme as that, but in a marriage, "failure to communicate" can be especially hurtful. One husband was overheard saying to his wife, "Honey, what do you mean we don't communicate? Just yesterday I texted you a reply to the voicemail you left me!" That's communication for you.

Still, it's amazing how a husband and wife who are trying to communicate can talk right past each other. What a wife says may translate into something entirely different for her husband. Likewise, what he says may mean something else to his wife. When a couple is driving somewhere and they get lost, she will say, "Let's ask for directions." But he hears, "You're not a man."

When she says, "Can I have the remote control?" he hears, "Let's watch something that will bore you beyond belief!"

She tells him, "You need to get in touch with your feelings."

He hears, *"Blah, blah, blah."*

She asks, "Are you listening to me?"

He hears, *"Blah, blah, blah, blah, blah."*

She says, "I'd like to redecorate."

He hears, *"Let's take our money and flush it down the toilet."*

What we have here is a failure to communicate! But we have to keep trying, don't we?

Not only should we be quick to listen, James tells us, but we should also be slow to get angry. As Proverbs 29:11 tells us, "Fools vent their anger, but the wise quietly hold it back" (NLT).

Don't let anger control your life. Don't let it have a place in your marriage.

I heard about a husband and wife who, as newlyweds, decided to put into practice Ephesians 4:26, which says, "Be angry, and do not sin: do not let the sun go down on your wrath" (NKJV). So, they determined never to go to bed mad at each other. Thirty years later, someone asked the husband how it worked out. He replied, "Pretty well, but sometimes it was a little rough sitting up all night."

Yet there are certain people who are always mad about something. They never seem to be happy unless they are mad. They get over one thing and move on to another. They're always griping or complaining about something. The problem is that people who are often angry become bitter people. Bitter people rarely keep it to themselves. They want to spread it around.

If you or your spouse fits this description, beware. It will infect your marriage and can also spread to your children and to others in your life. The Bible warns about a root of bitterness that can spring up and defile many (see Hebrews 12:15). Don't let bitterness overtake your marriage.

Have you been wronged? Has someone hurt you? Has someone said something unkind about you? Perhaps it was your spouse. You need to forgive him or her. "But they don't deserve it," you say. Regardless of what someone has said or done to us, the Bible tells us, "And be kind to one another, tenderhearted, forgiving one another, even as God in Christ forgave you" (Ephesians 4:32 NKJV).

You should extend forgiveness because God has extended forgiveness to you. When you forgive someone, you set a prisoner free: *yourself.* When you harbor bitterness, you are hurting yourself. You are hurting other people. You aren't helping anything.

Let it go. Forgive. Put it behind you. Don't carry it any further.

Thinking Before We Speak

In addition to being slow to get angry, we should be slow to speak, which is really the thrust of what James is saying in these verses. A major part of self-control is mouth control.

It's difficult to put your foot in your mouth when it's closed. That's something to think about. If we just would be quick to listen and slow to speak, we would avoid so much unnecessary misery. The Bible teaches that one day we will be held accountable for what we have said.

Jesus said, "But I say to you that for every idle word men may speak, they will give account of it in the day of judgment. For by your words you will be justified, and by your words you will be condemned" (Matthew 12:36–37 NKJV).

Most of us speak a great many words in the course of our lives. It has been estimated that people speak enough words in one week to fill a 500-page book. But a true test of your faith is not the ability to speak your mind, but to hold your tongue. James is saying that if you want to be a spiritually mature person, you'll do it by learning to control your words. That is why the psalmist said, "I will watch what I do and not sin in what I say. I will hold my tongue when the ungodly are around me" (Psalm 39:1 NLT). We need to think about what we say, because there are many ways we can misuse our words.

Here is something to THINK about when you are talking to your husband, wife, or anyone, for that matter. When you are in doubt about something you're about to say, apply this test:

T   Is it *true?*

H   Is it *helpful?*

I   Is it *inspiring?*

N   Is it *necessary?*

K   Is it *kind?*

You might be saying, "Give me a break! If I applied these standards, I'd have to eliminate 90 percent of what I say!"

Then so be it.

Understand, even godly men and women struggle with keeping this area under control. Some of the greatest people that God ever used struggled with it. So don't feel like you're the only one.

Take Job, for instance. God Himself called Job "blameless" (Job 1:8 NLT). Yet even Job had trouble controlling his own tongue. He said, "I am nothing—how could I ever find the answers? I will cover my mouth with my hand. I have said too much already" (Job 40:4 NLT).

Isaiah was one of God's choice servants, but when he came into God's presence, the first things he became aware of were his words—and how he used his tongue. He said, "Woe is me, for I am undone! Because I am a man of unclean lips, and I dwell in the midst of a people of unclean lips; for my eyes have seen the King, the Lord of hosts" (Isaiah 6:5 NKJV). When Isaiah was in the presence of God, he immediately became aware of the fact that he had misused his words and his tongue.

Using Our Words Wisely

When a toddler throws a fit for no apparent reason, screaming unintelligibly, we often say, "Use your words." We want them to communicate clearly and express their feelings calmly. This is a good reminder for us as well. Instead of demanding things of others, including our spouses, we should "use our words" clearly, calmly, and wisely. But how?

1. We should use our words to glorify God

Glorifying God is the highest and greatest use of our tongue because we were created to glorify God and give Him pleasure. The apostle James notes: "With the tongue we praise our Lord and Father, and with it we curse human beings, who have been made in God's likeness. Out of the same mouth come praise and cursing. My brothers and sisters, this should not be" (James 3:9–10 NIV).

It's important to remember that we were put on this earth to bring honor and praise to the One who created us—and one of the ways we can accomplish that is through what we say.

Scripture overflows with examples of verbal praise to God. David wrote, "Because Your lovingkindness is better than life, my lips shall praise You. Thus I will bless You while I live; I will lift up my hands in Your name" (Psalm 63:3–4 NKJV).

Ephesians 5:18–19 tells us, "Be filled with the Holy Spirit, singing psalms and hymns and spiritual songs among yourselves, and making music to the Lord in your hearts" (NLT).

2. We should use our words to build up our spouse

I believe the Lord wants us to reevaluate how we use our words with our spouse. Let's use them for the right reasons. Let's compliment, not criticize. Let's speak authentically, not manipulatively. Let's use our words with the intention of building up, not tearing down. Let's ask God to give us the strength in our marriages to use our words in the most loving, encouraging ways.

The Bible says, "Let no corrupt word proceed out of your mouth, but what is good for necessary edification, that it may impart grace to the hearers" (Ephesians 4:29 NKJV).

Keep in mind, it's not only *what* we say that's important, but it's *how* we say it. Our tone can speak volumes to our spouse, either building them up tenderly, or tearing them down harshly.

3. We should use our words to shape our children

If you don't instruct your children or give them a spiritual foundation, they will likely depart from the faith. As parents, let's be the ones to say, "Hey, let's read some Bible stories together. Let's do a little study together. Let's spend some time in prayer."

In the case of Joshua, he didn't say, "As for me and my house, I hope that we will follow the Lord." No. He said, "As for me and my house, we will serve the LORD" (Joshua 24:15 NKJV).

Our words should lovingly, but firmly, teach, instruct, and shape our children.

> Jonathan's Perspective: I want to emphasize the importance of forgiveness. There are times I have lost my temper with my wife. I have said things that I didn't mean. I have done things in front of my kids that I shouldn't have done. And they have witnessed that. They know that I'm a pastor at church, that I have a higher standard to live up to as a result of that.
>
> So, guess what I do? I deal with it head-on. I go straight to my kids and tell them, "You know what? Dad blew it. I should not have done that. I'm sorry. Will you forgive me?"

And I'll be the first to tell you this resonates with my kids probably more than anything I've taught them. It's not easy to go and tell your kids that you're sorry. Right? We as parents want to be right. "Because I said so." These are my favorite four words in the world.

But we have to make sure that we humble ourselves and are real with our kids. We can't pretend that we're perfect. We can't pretend that we have it all figured out because there's only one Person who ever fit that criteria: Jesus Christ

So, strive to be a better parent, and apologize

4. We should use our words to reach people

As we come into contact with people like our neighbors, coworkers, people at the gym, or someone at a restaurant, how can we use our words to reach them, to share our faith?

Well, it starts with learning their name, right?

We can invest a little time in learning more about them—what they like or dislike, what they do for a living, what they're going through. We can make mental notes (or notes on our phone) to reach out to them. It can be as simple as this: "I just want to let you know I'm thinking about you, and I'm praying for you," or "If there's anything I can do for you, please let me know."

You never know how a few genuine words will impact someone's life.

We need to build bridges to earn people's trust. Look at it this way: If you don't know anything about your neighbors, not even their names, and you don't befriend them or serve them in any way, why would they listen to you when it comes to your faith? Why would they care what you believe?

It's been said, "People don't care how much you know until they know how much you care." Share what God has done for you. Talk about it. Live out your faith.

Reaching people starts with befriending them. Being there for them. Running to help when needed.

I like to summarize it this way: Upward, inward, outward. *Upward* is the glorification of God. *Inward* is the edification of the saints. And *outward* is the evangelization of the world. This is what our mission is as Christians. This is what our mission is as the church.

We're not a political movement seeking personal gain. No. We (the church) are people from every walk of life—every continent, every tongue, every race, every age, every stage—proclaiming that Jesus Christ is Lord and sharing that with an unsaved and broken world.

There is incredible power in our words, to encourage, build up, strengthen, forgive, and share the mighty love of God. Let's be the ones to use our words for God's glory and the good of others. Amen?

Prayer: Lord, You tell us in Your Word that "the tongue can bring death or life." Help us speak words of life to everyone we encounter. To our spouses, children, coworkers, neighbors, and strangers, give us words of truth and grace. Please soften our tone, removing the harshness and replacing it with tenderness and mercy. Let every word we speak be spoken in love, Your love. In the name of Jesus and for His sake, amen.

QUESTIONS for Discussion

1. Why is the tongue "the world's most dangerous weapon"?

2. This chapter says, "Most of us can remember hurtful words and taunts from the earliest days of childhood. Years and decades may roll by, but simply recalling those harsh or degrading words has the power to bring pain to the soul." Is that true for you? Can you recall negative or demeaning words spoken to you as a child or young person that you remember to this day? Now, to view the other side of this issue, can you remember positive, encouraging words someone spoke to you that you have treasured through your life?

3. James writes: "My dear brothers and sisters, take note of this: Everyone should be quick to listen, slow to speak and slow to become angry" (James 1:19 NIV). What does it mean to be "quick to listen"? What steps can we take to improve in that area?

4. What about the biblical counsel to be "slow to speak"? What habits or practices would you need to change to follow this advice? What additional insights can we gather from Proverbs 18:13 and 29:20?

5. The Bible teaches that one day we will be held accountable for what we have said. How does this encourage you to think before you speak? How does it remind you to soften your tone, and be careful how you say things?

6. Unresolved anger that is allowed to fester may soon to turn to bitterness of heart. What does Hebrews 12:15 say in warning about bitterness? How can we remove these harmful feelings from our marriage relationship?

7. The Bible commands us to "be kind to one another, tenderhearted, forgiving one another, even as God in Christ forgave you" (Ephesians 4:32 NKJV). What are some truths or characteristics about the way God forgave us in Christ? How then do we forgive others in the same way?

8. It was said in this chapter, "Glorifying God is the highest and greatest use of our tongue because we were created to glorify God and give Him pleasure." How can this powerful truth compel us to speak words that are honorable to the Lord, even when we're angry or dealing with conflict?

9. This chapter said, "It's difficult to put your foot in your mouth when it's closed." Jesus was more specific when He said, "But I say to you that for every idle word men may speak, they will give account of it in the day of judgment. For by your words you will be justified, and by your words you will be condemned" (Matthew 12:36–37 NKJV). If we really stopped to consider the above Scripture, how might it change the course of our comments and conversation in the course of a day?

10. Ephesians 4:29 says, "Let no corrupt word proceed out of your mouth, but what is good for necessary edification, that it may impart grace to the hearers" (NKJV). Are you in the habit of cursing or

using foul language in your home or workplace? If so, how can this passage help you change your thinking and begin speaking words of edification and grace?

11. This chapter said, "Our words should lovingly, but firmly, teach, instruct, and shape our children." Jonathan included the importance of apology and forgiveness. How easy is it for you to apologize to your children? How can you lay down feelings of pride or control and ask for forgiveness? What are some potential blessings of humbling yourself in front of your children?

12. Hebrews 13:15 says, "Therefore by Him let us continually offer the sacrifice of praise to God, that is, the fruit of our lips, giving thanks to His name" (NKJV). What do you think about the writer's use of the word *continually*? How do we continually offer praise to God throughout our day? How might we accomplish that?

13. This chapter closes with these powerful words: "We (the church) are people from every walk of life—every continent, every tongue, every race, every age, every stage—proclaiming that Jesus Christ is Lord, and sharing this with an unsaved and broken world." How does this reminder empower you to use your words for the sake of the gospel? In what way are you included in this great commission to reach the lost?

CHAPTER 8

Duty: The Forgotten Word

"Friends, don't slack off in doing your duty."
—2 Thessalonians 3:13 (MSG)

Once upon a time, there was a word that was animating, galvanizing, and strengthening to our forefathers and foremothers.

When spoken—whether to a king in his castle, a soldier in the field, or the scullery maid in the kitchen—they would have known exactly what you meant, and many would have nodded their heads in recognition.

If you use the word today, however, most people won't even know what you're talking about—or if they do, they won't care.

It is a word that has fallen on hard times.

The word is *duty*, and apart from emergency responders or military members, it's not a term that most of us think about in the 21st century.

But maybe we should.

And maybe we should think about that word, particularly in terms of marriage, family, and relationships.

It's been said, "A friend is one that walks in when others walk out." Are you a friend like that to someone? Or do you have a friend like that? A friendship is made up of two people committing themselves one to another. It can only exist where there is a response that needs to be reciprocal.

True friends support each other through thick and thin. They're consistent. Proverbs 17:17 says, "A friend loves at all times, and a brother is born for a time of adversity" (NIV).

We all need that kind of commitment, don't we? The kind that says, "I'm there for you, no matter what."

Sadly, we live in such self-absorbed times that the idea of doing something simply because it's the right thing to do has fallen out of favor. Nowadays the mentality is this:

What's right for ME?

What's in it for ME?

What about MY needs?

This is one of the reasons that marriages and families are so rapidly failing in our day. We'll say, "My mate no longer satisfies my needs. I'm no longer happy in this marriage." Then perhaps, we even have the temerity to drag God into it, saying, "God wants me to be happy. God wouldn't want me to stay in a marriage where I'm no longer fulfilled and content."

But wait a second. What about the commitment that you made? What about doing your duty as a Christian husband or wife? What about those vows that you stated to one another when you said you took that person for better or for worse, for richer or for poorer, in sickness and in health, to love and to cherish until death do you part?

Duty Is a Demand

The dictionary defines *duty* as "something that one is expected or required to do by moral or legal obligation."

Does that sound a bit harsh? Do you find words like *expected* or *required* hard to swallow? These words meant something different to people, even as few as 50 years ago.

It was Civil War General Robert E. Lee who wrote, "Duty then is the sublimest word in the English language. You should do your duty in all things. You can never do more. You should never wish to do less."

And the 19th-century preacher Henry Ward Beecher put it poetically: "He who is false to present duty breaks a thread in the loom, and will find the flaw when he may have forgotten its cause."

Then there's *The Book of Common Prayer* that speaks of daily life in these terms: "To do my duty in that state of life unto which it shall please God to call me."

Even Johann Goethe said, "What then is your duty? What the day demands."

Finally, an unknown individual offered these words that have somehow lasted through the years: "If I do my full duty, the rest will take care of itself."[14]

Duty might be a word that has fallen on deaf ears, but it's something that goes along with being a husband, wife, father, mother, or human being for that matter. And as Christians, we especially need to be reminded of our God-given duties.

Solomon penned these words in Ecclesiastes 12:13, saying, "Now all has been heard; here is the conclusion of the matter: Fear God and keep his commandments, for this is the duty of all mankind" (NIV).

Yet people don't seem to *want* to uphold their responsibilities anymore. They don't want to live in accountability to God or others. Instead, they feel as though the world owes *them* something.

Mark Twain said, "Don't go around saying the world owes you a living. The world owes you nothing. It was here first."[15]

Just saying the word *duty* reminds me of jury duty. I have been called—and served—many times. A number of years ago, John, one of our associate pastors at Harvest Fellowship, received a summons to serve on jury duty. But he didn't want to go. He was busy, it wasn't convenient, and he didn't want to hassle with it. So he told me, "I'm just going to write them a letter and tell them I can't do it."

"John," I said, "you can't do that. You have to have a legitimate reason for avoiding jury duty. You can't just not show up. You have to contact the court and ask them for permission to be relieved." But John wouldn't believe it. Why should he be bothered? He didn't want to do it. He wrote his letter and said he was just too busy.

That's when I decided to play a little trick on John. We made arrangements with one of the Christian cops in our church to have John "arrested" for avoiding jury duty. It was all a joke, of course, but he didn't know that.

John came walking out of church one Sunday morning with a big smile on his face, and there waiting for him was a uniformed officer with the LAPD. With a face that was expressionless as a stone, this cop walked up to John and said, "Is your name [giving John's full name]?"

"Yes, it is," John said.

The policeman said, "I hereby place you under arrest for avoidance of your lawful jury duty."

John looked around, trying to find the joke. "This is a joke, right?"

But the L.A. cop actually put him against the car, put John's hands behind his back and cuffed him! I was watching all of this, of course, and beginning to wonder if it had all gone a little too far. I was actually starting to feel sorry for my friend. Then the policeman put him into the back of the squad car, and closed the door. And John wasn't smiling anymore.

I thought to myself, "I think it's time to put an end to this." So, I walked up to the policeman and said, "Excuse me, officer. But I think it's okay. We can stop this now."

The cop looked me square in the eyes and said, "You, back off."

I backed off.

For whatever reason, the LAPD officer kept John in the back of his squad car for 10 more minutes before finally releasing him with a little smile.

I think John will show up for jury duty next time!

Remember Whose ID Tag You're Wearing
In Luke 17, we have the call of our Lord to do our duty as Christians. The problem is, many of us are reluctant to embrace that word even when it's

Jesus who speaks it. And even when it applies to our relationship with the people we love most.

> Suppose one of you has a servant plowing or looking after the sheep. Will he say to the servant when he comes in from the field, "Come along now and sit down to eat"? Won't he rather say, "Prepare my supper, get yourself ready and wait on me while I eat and drink; after that you may eat and drink"? Will he thank the servant because he did what he was told to do? So you also, when you have done everything you were told to do, should say, "We are unworthy servants; we have only done our duty." (Luke 17:7–10 NIV)

We must remember that as Christians we are the purchased property of Jesus Christ. On more than one occasion, the Bible likens us to slaves. It's as if we were in an open slave market, and Jesus comes and bids for our freedom. He pays the price. Then He takes us into His own service. We were formerly slaves to sin under the power of Satan, the prince of the power of the air. But then Jesus purchased our freedom with His own blood. Now, we are to serve Him.

From the day that we put our faith in Jesus Christ, we became His purchased property. Amplifying on this theme, 1 Corinthians 6:20 says: "You were bought at a price; therefore glorify God in your body and in your spirit, which are God's" (NKJV).

For all practical purposes, when you became a Christian, God attached His ID tag to you. You are, in effect, wearing the ID tag of Christ. You are His. You belong to Him. You bear His name and His Word, so everything you do should reflect Him.

When I travel, I usually take a suitcase or two. I have a tendency to over pack and take too many things with me. When I go to the baggage carousel, my bag will inevitably be the last one to come down the chute. Even so, I always check the luggage tag. I don't want to be loading someone else's things into my car and driving home with them. But just one glance at that ID tag confirms that this piece of luggage belongs to me.

When you became a follower of Jesus Christ, He attached His ID tag to you. We can see this truth highlighted in Ephesians 1:13–14: "In Him you also trusted, after you heard the word of truth, the gospel of your salvation; in whom also, having believed, you were sealed with the Holy Spirit of promise, who is the guarantee of our inheritance until the redemption of the purchased possession, to the praise of His glory" (NKJV).

The passage says I have been "sealed with the Holy Spirit of promise." What does that mean? Back in biblical times, when goods were shipped from one place to another, they would be stamped with a wax seal imprinted with a signet ring bearing a unique mark of ownership. If you saw a crate that had a wax seal with the king's imprint, you certainly wouldn't want to mess with that. In fact, you'd want to avoid all appearance of interfering with that piece of cargo, because a violation might well mean your life.

In the same way, God has placed His very own imprint on our lives—His ID tag, if you will. I don't think we begin to understand what weight that carries in the universe. For instance, when the devil wants to come and make havoc of your life, he is stopped cold because he sees that seal of ownership.

Let's say you're a thief in an airport who wants to steal something, and you spot a very expensive briefcase on the conveyer belt. You look around, and nobody seems to be claiming the case. What a prize it would be! It has gold-plated hinges, and the handle is studded with diamonds. You say to yourself, "Wow, that case alone is valuable. Imagine what's in it!"

As you walk over to it, intending to quickly steal it and walk away, you notice an ID tag attached to it. It has the word "Tyson" on it.

You think, "Tyson? As in Tyson chicken?"

Then you see a very large, muscular man, half of his face tattooed, walking toward you, and you realize it's *Mike* Tyson, the professional fighter, who owns that briefcase. As a result, you decide to walk away and leave it alone. Why? Because you enjoy life. And you fear the owner.

In the same way, the devil—the one who has come "to steal, and to kill, and to destroy" (John 10:10 NKJV)—approaches you. In his hatred and malice, he says, "I will wreak havoc in this life. I will ruin this person. I'll . . .

wait, is that an ID tag? What does it say? 'Property of the Lord Jesus Christ? Purchased with His blood'? Uh-oh." And he backs off.

Satan does not have free rein to attack and destroy a son or daughter of God, because we have been sealed with the Holy Spirit of promise. God has put His ID tag on you, which is an incredible privilege.

But with that privilege comes responsibility.

Fulfilling Your Responsibilities

I raised two wonderful sons, including one who is now with the Lord. As my boys grew up, they had all the privileges that went with being the sons of Greg and Cathe Laurie. They had a roof over their heads, food, clothing, skateboards, and whatever they needed. They had open and free access to me whenever they wanted it. If they were in trouble, I would be there for them. They knew I was always in their corner. Those were the privileges that came with relationship, as sons to their dad.

With those privileges there were also some responsibilities. In fact, as the boys were growing up, I would often give them tasks and instruct them what to do. I wouldn't say, "Would you please—just for me—take out the trash?" No, as their dad, I simply told them to do this or that. And most of the time they did!

Why did I say it that way? Simply put, to get things done. We had a household to run, and each of us had a part to play. As a parent, I was responsible to see that as my boys grew up, they knew how to help, contribute, and carry their own weight. Besides that, we had a relationship. I could speak to them that way, because of the relationship of intimacy we already had as father and sons. They had no problem with getting simple marching orders from their dad; they expected it.

But I can't do that with a total stranger. I can't stop someone walking by my house and say, "Hey, you. Come in here and take out the trash." I'd like to, but I really can't do that, because I have no relationship with that person. But I had the right to tell my own sons what to do, and to expect them to do it.

In the same way here in our text, God addresses us as His sons and daughters. He is essentially saying, "As My own children, you have all of the privileges and perks that come with relationship. You have My presence. You have My blessing. You have open access to Me 24/7. But you also have responsibilities. As my children, there are certain things that I expect of you. I want you to do what I tell you to do."

This is what Jesus is saying in Luke 17:9, "And does the master thank the servant for doing what he was told to do? Of course not" (NLT).

No, He isn't obliged to do that. We belong to Him. We're His servants. We have responsibilities that are expected of us.

Here's another way to look at it: The very fact that Jesus would call upon us and tell us to do something should thrill our hearts. Why? Because it's a mark of ownership. He feels, and rightly so, that as your Father who has purchased your life with precious blood, He can call upon you to do something, and He expects your obedience. In essence, you have already agreed to this by accepting His salvation and forgiveness. You committed yourself to this when you said yes to Jesus Christ.

Interestingly, as you read many of Paul's New Testament letters, you'll see that he often opens with the phrase, "Paul, a servant of Jesus Christ." The word he uses for *servant* could better be translated as "bondslave." We may not understand the significance of that term, but they certainly did in the first century. A bondslave was a servant who had been freed, and then chose to serve willingly.

In other words, you're like that slave bought in the auction. You serve your master for seven years, then he lets you go. In response, you say, "Master, I love you so much that I don't want to leave you. I want to become your voluntary slave now. I want to be a bondslave." That would be indicated by a mark they would make in the lobe of your ear. From that time forward, anyone who saw you would know that you were a servant by choice—a voluntary slave to a master you loved more than your own life.

Paul would say, "I am a bondslave." The same is absolutely true of us, and there can be no quibbling or negotiating in this area. It is our duty to do what God tells us to do.

Let me add that a true follower of Jesus should *want* to do His will. As soon as he knows what it is, he should gladly jump in and do it. If you know the will of God, then as a Christian, you should be happy that you know it, and you should just get out and do it.

Romans 12:11 says, "Never be lazy, but work hard and serve the Lord enthusiastically" (NLT).

A friend of ours is now with the Lord. He was very involved at our Riverside campus, and had been part of our church family for about 30 years. At his memorial, his celebration of life, it was amazing to hear how he had fulfilled his God-given duties.

He never stood on the stage. He never preached a sermon. He never played a guitar or sang on the frontline, but you know what he did? He touched So. Many. Lives.

The church sanctuary was packed out, completely full of people. And after the service, every single person we spoke with had an amazing story of how this man had blessed their lives. How he was generous, how he met people's needs, how he was there for them when they fell into sin. He was always there to help pick them back up and restore them. Absolutely amazing. We need more men and women like this, to fulfill their God-given roles and responsibilities.

It's a Privilege

People will often write me very nice letters and emails and say complimentary things to me after a church service. (I also get mean or even threatening letters and emails. But the nice ones outnumber those by far.) People will say things like,

"Greg, I really appreciate what you do."

"Greg, I thank God that you preach the gospel and teach the Word."

"Thank you for your work, Greg. Thank you for your sacrifice."

Now those are nice words, and I appreciate being appreciated as much as anyone does. But the truth is, I'm only doing my duty just as you are doing your duty. None of us deserve any special thanks because we're doing what God has called us to do.

I'll let you in on a little secret, however. It is my great privilege and joy to do what I do. I enjoy it thoroughly. I take great delight in doing the duty that God has called me to do. And I hope you have the same attitude toward what He has called you to do.

Having established the fact that we are to do our duty, what is our duty specifically? In context of the chapters you have just completed, we have a duty to our marriage, and a duty to our family.

Doing the Right Thing

You say, "I still don't like that word 'duty.' I prefer to say that I have the privilege or the opportunity or the pleasure of caring for my spouse and staying faithful to my vows."

Yes, I would say the same thing.

But sometimes, when life gets pulled this way and that when we're feeling overwhelmed, undervalued, burned-out, or brokenhearted, when we can no longer feel much of anything and care even less, we still have a duty to our spouse and our children. We need to do the right thing by our family simply because it is the right thing.

Ultimately, we need to do it because we belong—heart, body, and soul—to Jesus Christ, and as our Lord, it's what He expects of us.

What sort of duties? I'm talking about the biblical imperatives we've talked about in this book:

- "Therefore be imitators of God as dear children. And walk in love, as Christ also has loved us and given Himself for us" (Ephesians 5:1–2 NKJV).
- "Wives, submit to your own husbands, as to the Lord" (Ephesians 5:22 NKJV).
- "Husbands, love your wives, just as Christ also loved the church and gave Himself for her" (Ephesians 5:25 NKJV).
- "Children, obey your parents in the Lord, for this is right" (Ephesians 6:1 NKJV).

- "Husbands, in the same way be considerate as you live with your wives, and treat them with respect as the weaker partner and as heirs with you of the gracious gift of life" (1 Peter 3:7 NIV).
- "Husbands, love your wives and do not be harsh with them" (Colossians 3:19 NIV).
- "And you, fathers, do not provoke your children to wrath, but bring them up in the training and admonition of the Lord" (Ephesians 6:4 NKJV).
- "Submit to one another out of reverence for Christ" (Ephesians 5:21 NIV).
- "Nevertheless let each one of you in particular so love his own wife as himself" (Ephesians 5:33 NKJV).
- "Let the wife see that she respects her husband" (Ephesians 5:33 NKJV).
- "The husband should fulfill his marital duty to his wife, and likewise the wife to her husband. The wife does not have authority over her own body but yields it to her husband. In the same way, the husband does not have authority over his own body but yields it to his wife" (1 Corinthians 7:3–4 NIV).
- "Anyone who does not provide for their relatives, and especially for their own household, has denied the faith and is worse than an unbeliever" (1 Timothy 5:8 NIV).

What, then, are these commands? Are they incredible privileges or duties? The answer is that they're both. And they're still duties even when they don't feel like privileges! We need to love and provide and protect and submit and cherish and respect our mates because Jesus expects us to.

You don't want to? You don't feel like it? You're not motivated?

So what?

Do those things anyway, as unto Jesus. The One who shed His blood for you and laid down His life for you has every right to expect full-hearted obedience. God has called us to a certain way of living in every area of our lives—living for Him.

But I want to share that the reason God is worth living for is not because He's some distant deity, or some creator out in the cosmos that we don't know. No. The reason that He is worth living for is because the deepest sense of fulfillment and joy and love and peace and forgiveness and purpose is through knowing Him as your God, your Savior, and your friend.

Here's a little secret: The more you do for your family, and as unto Him, the sweeter life becomes. Happiness slips in through the back door, and stays a long, long time.

Prayer: Lord, please forgive us for failing to live up to our duties and responsibilities. It's become easy to be lazy and make excuses, but You call us to something more. We bear the name of Jesus on our ID tags, meaning we reflect Him in everything we say and do. Please hold us to this standard, reminding us often of the sacrifice He gave for each of us. Fill us with joy in serving You and others, and give us renewed purpose and strength. We recommit ourselves to You, Lord. In Jesus' name, amen.

QUESTIONS for Discussion

1. What would your first impression of the word *duty* have been, had you not read through this chapter? Would it have seemed like an outdated word, or something irrelevant to your life?

2. It was said, "We live in such self-absorbed times that the idea of doing something simply because it's the right thing to do has fallen out of favor. Nowadays the mentality is, 'What's right for ME? What's in it for ME? What about MY needs?'" Do you agree with this statement? What evidence of this attitude have you seen within yourself or others in the last few weeks?

3. Some people argue: "God wants me to be happy. God wouldn't want me to stay in a marriage where I'm no longer fulfilled and content." If one of your friends or loved ones was in an immoral relationship and came to you with the above argument, how would you counter it? What Scriptures might you use?

4. There are duties that go along with being a husband or a wife, a father or a mother. Does the word *duty* make you think of drudgery—or privilege and opportunity? How much are we influenced

by our contemporary culture as we seek to process this concept of
duty?

5. Read Luke 17:7–10. What do you think the Lord wants us to learn
    from these verses? What wrong or harmful heart attitude might the
    Lord be addressing with these words?

6. "From the day that we put our faith in Jesus Christ, we became His
    purchased property." How does this resonate with you? Are you at all
    offended by the phrase "purchased property"? What does the Lord
    remind us of in 1 Corinthians 6:20? "For God bought you with a
    high price. So you must honor God with your body" (NLT).

7. Read Ephesians 1:13–14. What are the implications of wearing the
    Lord Jesus' ID tag? List as many examples of reflecting Christ as
    you can.

8. This chapter states, "Satan does not have free rein to attack and de-
    stroy a son or daughter of God, because we have been sealed with
    the Holy Spirit of promise. God has put His ID tag on you, which is
    an incredible privilege." How does this comfort you knowing you're
    protected and sealed by the Holy Spirit? What are the responsibilities
    that go along with this privilege?

9. Because the Father purchased our lives at the cost of His Son's pre-
    cious blood, He has a full right to expect our obedience. In essence
    He's saying that you have already agreed to this by accepting His
    salvation and forgiveness. How would you apply this truth to your
    marriage, and the specific directions for wives and husbands that we
    have seen in this book?

10. Ultimately, we need to carefully follow the Bible's instructions as
    husbands and wives because we belong—heart, body, and soul—to
    Jesus Christ. It's what He expects of us. So, how can we make sure our
    obedience to Christ is a choice of the heart, as well as an expectation
    and a duty?

CHAPTER 9

Wise and Godly Friendships

"The man of too many friends [chosen indiscriminately] will be broken in pieces and come to ruin, but there is a [true, loving] friend who [is reliable and] sticks closer than a brother." —Proverbs 18:24 (AMP)

Two men camping in the forest were enjoying their morning coffee when they suddenly spotted a very large, hungry grizzly bear running toward them. One of the men quickly pulled on his running shoes.

"Do you actually think you can outrun that grizzly bear?" his friend asked.

"I don't need to," he replied. "All I have to do is outrun you."

We've all had friends like this, haven't we? At the first threat of danger, hardship, or difficulty, they're out the back door.

We must give serious consideration to the people we spend our free time with and the people we bare our hearts to. The apostle Paul warned, "Bad company corrupts good character" (1 Corinthians 15:33 NIV). This means you will be influenced by the people you hang out with, and they will be influenced by you.

Paul also wrote, "Run from anything that stimulates youthful lusts. Instead, pursue righteous living, faithfulness, love, and peace. Enjoy the companionship of those who call on the Lord with pure hearts" (2 Timothy 2:22 NLT).

So, what makes for true friendship?

Sociologists tell us that in the first stage of life, we are shaped mostly by our family. In the second stage of life, and for the rest of our lives, we are shaped largely by our friends. Show me your friends, and I'll show you your future.

In big ways and small, we become like the people we spend time with. Our friends influence us for better or worse. They either elevate us and motivate us to be our best possible selves, or they take us down with them.

Proverbs 18:24 distinguishes between destructive friends and real friends, saying, "There are 'friends' who destroy each other, but a real friend sticks closer than a brother" (NLT).

In real life, however, it's sometimes hard to tell the difference between friends "who destroy" and friends who stick "closer than a brother." And if you don't have a lot of friends, it's hard to tell whether a friend who destroys is worse than no friend at all. Can you relate?

One of the greatest friendships in history defines what it means to be a true and wise friend. It's found in 1 Samuel 18 and introduces us to the unlikely friendship of David and Jonathan.

In case you're not familiar with these two, Jonathan was the son of King Saul, king of Israel. David was anointed to take Saul's place even though Jonathan was next in line. Think about how this could have turned out. It could have easily turned into a revenge story—Jonathan's plot to kill David in order to take the throne. But Jonathan saw something more. He saw a true friend in David and supported him from the beginning.

First Samuel 18:1-3 says, "After David had finished talking with Saul, he met Jonathan, the king's son. There was an immediate bond between them, for Jonathan loved David. From that day on Saul kept David with him and wouldn't let him return home. And Jonathan made a solemn pact with David, because he loved him as he loved himself" (NLT).

The Bible does not back away from the fact that David and Jonathan had deep love for each other, and that love was not, as some say, weird in any way. It was *phileo*—friendship love, that is rare, powerful, and so precious.

I have heard that on average, we maintain some degree of connection with 150 people at any given time in life, but only about 12 are people we consider to be personal friends. Of those 12, two or three might be considered "besties." When it comes to lifetime friendships, the deepest level of love and commitment is rare.

When we read of the *phileo* friendship between Jonathan and David, we see how united they were in the pursuit of something beyond themselves. It was a passion that captured them first, as individuals, then as a united front in pursuing God and His glory. When each one recognized this virtue in the other, it forged their friendship into an unbreakable bond.

Jonathan and David made a covenant, not only to each other, but to God. Jonathan recognized God's will and calling on David's life, even though it meant he would not be king. This brings us to our first point.

A Wise Friend Recognizes God's Will

Imagine how Jonathan felt when he learned that David would succeed his father. Here was this shepherd boy who wrote poetry, chosen to take the throne. The Bible doesn't tell us how Jonathan reacted, but we do know from history that princes and shepherds did not mix. They didn't form close friendships. One was considered part of the elite, while the other was considered the underbelly of society.

However, Jonathan recognized God's will and graciously stepped aside. He became a support system for David, preferring him above himself. He was, in effect, living out Philippians 2:3, which says, "Let nothing be done through selfish ambition or conceit, but in lowliness of mind let each esteem others better than himself" (NKJV).

Now, did Jonathan struggle? Did he wrestle with the fact that his future plans as king had changed? We don't know for sure, but what we do know is this: He submitted to God's will. Not only did he submit to God's will, but he also made sacrifices for David to step into his anointed role. This is what a wise friend does.

A wise friend is willing to yield, as James 3:17 says, "But the wisdom from above is first of all pure. It is also peace loving, gentle at all times, and willing to yield to others. It is full of mercy and the fruit of good deeds. It shows no favoritism and is always sincere" (NLT). Jonathan represented all of these virtues, seeking peace instead of division and mercy instead of revenge.

Despite the easy road, the one promising a secure future, Jonathan chose the will of God. In fact, he went in the opposite direction of his father, Saul, which was rather risky. First Samuel 19:1–3 paints the picture, saying, "Saul now urged his servants and his son Jonathan to assassinate David. But Jonathan, because of his strong affection for David, told him what his father was planning. "Tomorrow morning," he warned him, "you must find a hiding place out in the fields. I'll ask my father to go out there with me, and I'll talk to him about you. Then I'll tell you everything I can find out" (NLT).

Talk about a faithful friend! Jonathan was committed to God and was faithful to what God had called him to do. Instead of floating along, being carried with the current of Saul's plans, Jonathan swam upstream.

Christian apologist and writer, G. K. Chesterton, once said, "A dead thing can go with the stream, but only a living thing can go against it."[16]

Jonathan had the choice to follow his father's will or God's will, and he chose the better way. In our friendships, we will face spiritual forks in the road. We will have to make decisions that aren't easy. And most of the time, it will come down to God's will or our own. We'll be tempted to choose what's comfortable, safe, and nonconfrontational. We'll be tempted to compromise.

As a believer, you might have a nonbelieving friend, and that's great. You have a divine opportunity to show the love of Jesus to them. But what happens when that friend starts to influence you negatively, pressuring you to do things you know aren't right? There's a good chance you'll need to make a tough decision: to stand on biblical principles or cave to temptation.

From experience, I can tell you that if you compromise you will be let down. But when you choose God's way, you will be blessed. Psalm 37:4–8 says,

> "Delight yourself also in the LORD, and He shall give you the desires of your heart. Commit your way to the LORD, trust also in Him, and He shall bring it to pass. He shall bring forth your

righteousness as the light, and your justice as the noonday. Rest in the LORD, and wait patiently for Him; do not fret because of him who prospers in his way, because of the man who brings wicked schemes to pass. Cease from anger, and forsake wrath; Do not fret—it only causes harm" (NKJV).

Jonathan didn't fret over what was to come. He delighted himself in the Lord and committed his future to an all-knowing God. A wise friend recognizes God's will and submits to it, even if it goes against cultural norms. This brings us to our next point.

A Wise Friend Is Countercultural

Today, the cultural norm is upside down. The things we once saw as virtues are now vices. The things we once celebrated are now mocked. And the things we once called "bad" are now declared "good."

Everything is upside down.

It takes courage and commitment to be a follower of Jesus. Wimps need not apply. So, if you want to march in lockstep with the culture and think what everyone tells you to think, then go for it. You'll probably be really popular and have lots of so-called friends.

But time after time, Jesus taught us to be countercultural. Think of the Sermon on the Mount when He said, "God blesses those who are humble, for they will inherit the whole earth. God blesses those who hunger and thirst for justice, for they will be satisfied" (Matthew 5:5–6 NLT).

Humility? Justice? These are countercultural by definition, aren't they? Yet Jonathan and David had a strong successful friendship because they did things differently. Their faith in God superseded what was expected from the culture.

The Bible says to forgive your enemies and to love them. It even says to give them food if they're hungry! It's hard to believe, but it's true. Romans 12:20–21 says, "If your enemies are hungry, feed them. If they are thirsty, give them something to drink. In doing this, you will heap burning coals of shame on their heads. Don't let evil conquer you, but conquer evil by doing good" (NLT).

As believers, we are called to live in a countercultural way. We constantly have to remind ourselves that when things don't seem normal, right, or good, we can always trust an unknown future to a known God. As you read this, you might be thinking:

God, this doesn't make sense to me.

I don't understand why You're calling me to do this.

It's not easy to go against the cultural norms.

But at the end of the day, you can trust God with every uncertain outcome. And that's what Jonathan did. His once-secure future as king was now uncertain, but his faith in God was more important than what the culture, or his father, Saul, demanded.

Now, I have some friends who aren't Christians, and I've maintained these friendships over the years. My continual hope is to move them toward Christ and be a good influence on them. Perhaps you have unbelieving friends as well, but listen, your close friends—the ones you confide in and spend the most time with—should be wise, godly people.

Find godly friends, and be a godly friend for someone else. And if any of your friends are dragging you down, it might be time to part company.

Abraham had this problem with his nephew Lot, who was such a spiritual drag that Uncle Abraham finally told him, "Hey, buddy, we need to part company. You go your way, and I'll go mine." Genesis 13:11 says, "So Lot chose for himself the whole plain of the Jordan and set out toward the east. The two men parted company" (NIV).

Sometimes, we have to part company with friends who are not good for us, who bring us down instead of build us up. This brings us to another important point.

A Wise Friend Builds You Up

I once heard the story of a fisherman who caught crabs and put them in a pail with no lid. Someone asked him, "Why don't you have a lid on your little pail so that the crabs can't get out?" He replied, "Oh, that's no problem. The moment the first crab tries to escape, the others reach up and pull him down."

This can happen in our spiritual lives as well. There are certain people who will bring you down spiritually. They don't like you to talk about your faith, but they like to tell dirty jokes or slander people. And after you hang out with them for a while, it brings you down.

Jonathan could have easily brought David down. After all, his father, Saul, was on a mission to take David out. But the Bible says Jonathan "strengthened his hand in God." This powerful encounter is found in 1 Samuel 23:15–18.

> So David saw that Saul had come out to seek his life. And David was in the Wilderness of Ziph in a forest. Then Jonathan, Saul's son, arose and went to David in the woods and strengthened his hand in God. And he said to him, "Do not fear, for the hand of Saul my father shall not find you. You shall be king over Israel, and I shall be next to you. Even my father Saul knows that." So the two of them made a covenant before the LORD. And David stayed in the woods, and Jonathan went to his own house. (NKJV)

Jonathan went into the wilderness to meet David where he was. This could have been seen as treason or aiding the enemy. But again, Jonathan cared more about his friend than himself. And he didn't give David a pep talk, saying things like:

You can do it; you got this.

I can pull some strings with my dad.

You just need to pull yourself up by your bootstraps.

No. Jonathan didn't try to solve David's problems; he directed his attention back to God. Now that's a good friend. A wise friend reminds you of what God has done. In David's life, God had plucked him out of obscurity, delivered a giant into his hands, and anointed him king of Israel. Jonathan built David up by pointing him in the right direction.

The right word at the right time is such an encouragement. As Proverbs 25:11 says, "Timely advice is lovely, like golden apples in a silver basket" (NLT). This isn't about painting a happy face on every situation and pretending everything's great. No. The best advice from a friend directs our attention to what God has done and will do.

> Jonathan's Story: A friend of mine who was a youth pastor in San Juan Capistrano used to reach out to me all the time. He'd call, text, and bug me to have lunch with him. I made excuses, saying things like, "I only get a 30-minute lunch break, so it's not gonna work." But he persisted and finally wore me down. He met me at work, we grabbed lunch at the drive-through, and we ate in my car.
>
> During that half-hour lunch, he encouraged me to go to church, read my Bible, and start walking with Jesus. He prayed for me and went on his way. And you know what? I eventually started going to his mid-week Bible study. He truly cared when I needed a friend the most. And in the aftermath of my brother going to Heaven, he was there for me. Like Jonathan in the Bible, he strengthened my hand in the Lord.

Psalm 27:1–3 gives us insight into what David was thinking after Jonathan encouraged him. David said, "The LORD is my light and my salvation—whom shall I fear? The LORD is the stronghold of my life—of whom shall I be afraid? When the wicked advance against me to devour me, it is my enemies and my foes who will stumble and fall. Though an army besiege me, my heart will not fear; though war break out against me, even then I will be confident" (NIV).

Finally, David ends the psalm with, "I remain confident of this: I will see the goodness of the LORD in the land of the living. Wait for the LORD; be strong and take heart and wait for the LORD" (Psalm 27:13–14 NIV).

A Wise Friend Speaks Truth

An enemy will flatter you and tell you to your face that you're great. But behind your back, the same person will cut you down. The Bible mentions this very thing in Proverbs 27:6, saying, "Wounds from a sincere friend are better than many kisses from an enemy" (NLT).

Sincere friends will say, "Because I love you, because I care about you, I must share this with you. I think you're making a mistake. I don't think you should do this." When friends truly care about you, they will tell you the truth.

So, how do you know the difference between an acquaintance and a friend? Friends are the ones you call on to share what you're going through. You share both joys and burdens. You let them into your life, through thick and thin.

Proverbs 27:9 says, "The heartfelt counsel of a friend is as sweet as perfume" (NLT).

I'm not talking about someone who always has an opinion and makes you feel bad about yourself. I'm talking about a friend who listens well and offers wise counsel as God leads. They are for you, not against you.

And don't forget that God is your friend. He always tells the truth. In fact, He wants to reveal His secrets to you. In Psalm 25:14 we read, "The secret of the LORD is with those who fear Him" (NKJV).

Jesus said, "My sheep hear My voice, and I know them, and they follow Me" (John 10:27 NKJV).

By the way, sheep are among the dumbest of all creatures. Most animals will survive if released into the wild. They will learn to fend for themselves and make it. But a sheep released into the wild cannot survive. Sheep have no survival skills whatsoever. They are totally dependent upon the shepherd—just like we are. The sheep know that when the shepherd speaks, they should follow, because his plan for them is best.

Wise friends will speak truth and point you to the Good Shepherd. They will have your best in mind. They will know when to speak up and when to remain silent.

In John 10:11–12, Jesus said, "I am the good shepherd. The good shepherd sacrifices his life for the sheep. A hired hand will run when he sees a wolf coming. He will abandon the sheep because they don't belong to him and he isn't their shepherd" (NLT). This is a great word picture of true friends who are sacrificial versus friends who scatter when trials come. And this brings us to our next point.

A Wise Friend Is Sacrificial

Let's take another look at 1 Samuel 18:1–4. "Now when he had finished speaking to Saul, the soul of Jonathan was knit to the soul of David, and Jonathan loved him as his own soul. Saul took him that day, and would not let him go home to his father's house anymore. Then Jonathan and David made a covenant, because he loved him as his own soul. And Jonathan took off the robe that was on him and gave it to David, with his armor, even to his sword and his bow and his belt" (NKJV).

Keep in mind, this encounter was right after David conquered Goliath. Jonathan saw something remarkable in David. He probably thought, "This guy just conquered the giant everyone was scared of. This scrawny teenager just defeated a mountain of a man. This is a friend I'd like to have."

It's interesting to note that Jonathan himself was a brave warrior. In 1 Samuel 14:12–14, we read,

"Jonathan said to his armorbearer, 'Come up after me, for the Lord has delivered them into the hand of Israel.' And Jonathan climbed up on his hands and knees with his armorbearer after him; and they fell before Jonathan. And as he came after him, his armorbearer killed them. That first slaughter which Jonathan and his armorbearer made was about twenty men within about half an acre of land" (NKJV).

Jonathan was a strong warrior and would've made a good king. His leadership would have been far better than his father, Saul's. But Jonathan was willing to sacrifice his own status and future for David, and ultimately, for the Lord.

Taking off his royal robe, his armor, and his sword symbolized Jonathan's willingness to sacrifice for his friend. He put David's needs and safety above his own, even though it could have cost him everything. Sacrificial love is the best kind of love a friend could have.

I once heard an amazing story about a young man, a Navy Seal named Mikey Monsoor. He was with his platoon on a rooftop after a gunfight in

Ramadi, Iraq. They got cornered and quickly called for reinforcements. But civilians from the surrounding towns were blocking the roadways and other soldiers weren't able to get in.

Then, in a surprising turn of events, the local mosques used loudspeakers to call every able-bodied person to come and fight the infidels who were cornering the Navy Seals on the rooftop.

Mikey and the others hunkered down, enduring heavy enemy fire. And just when they thought things couldn't get any worse, Mikey stood up near the stairwell and got hit in the chest with a live grenade. It bounced off his chest and landed on the ground. And in that moment, he had a choice to make. He could either dive into the stairwell and save himself or sacrifice his own life for others. In a split-second decision, Mikey yelled, "Grenade!" and then dove on top of it to absorb the explosion. He sacrificed himself for his friends and everyone nearby.

This is the type of love we see demonstrated in what Jesus did for us on the cross. In John 15:13, Jesus said, "Greater love hath no man than this, that a man lay down his life for his friends" (KJV).

What do these friendships reveal? As we look at David and Jonathan, we see that the love Jonathan had for David was a mere reflection of the type of love Jesus has for us. Yes, Jonathan gave up his right to the throne to support the Lord's anointed. But Jesus came down from Heaven, stripping Himself of royalty, to save the world.

Philippians 2:5–8 says,

> "Let this mind be in you which was also in Christ Jesus, who, being in the form of God, did not consider it robbery to be equal with God, but made Himself of no reputation, taking the form of a bondservant, and coming in the likeness of men. And being found in appearance as a man, He humbled Himself and became obedient to the point of death, even the death of the cross" (NKJV).

Jesus demonstrated selfless love throughout his earthly ministry, washing the feet of sinners, coming to serve and not be served, and most of all, laying down his life for us. Both Jonathan and Jesus made covenants. Jonathan's was to support David, protect his family, and help him take his rightful place as king. The Lord Jesus established a covenant with us, shedding His sinless blood on the cross, offering eternal life and forgiveness to all who believe in Him.

In Psalm 22:1, David prophesied, "My God, my God, why have you forsaken me?" (NIV). When Jesus repeated these words on the cross, it was a moment that theologians believe God turned His face away. For the very first time in all of eternity, the Father, Son, and Holy Spirit were splintered.

This is sacrificial love and the greatest friendship we could ever have. As we consider what types of friends to have, let's also think about what kind of friend we are.

Not Only Seeking, but Being a Wise Friend
Not only do we want to seek godly friendships, but we want to be the godly friend in our relationships. This means praying for our friends, staying informed about their struggles, and encouraging them with words of comfort, motivation, and wisdom from Scripture.

Your friends deserve genuine effort on your part. They need you to do the heavy lifting when they're hurting. Refuse to allow minor squabbles to grow into bigger problems by keeping the lines of communication open. Try to be quick to understand and even quicker to forgive. Be the person who sticks closer than a brother, no matter what happens.

The best place to cultivate godly friendships is where God's people meet. Worshiping or serving together in ministry is the ideal common ground on which to build a relationship. Instead of looking online for connection, try showing up in person. Find a Bible-believing church that has thriving small groups where you can get plugged in. Let the Bible be your guide, offering wisdom for finding godly friends and avoiding ungodly ones. Here are a few verses to remember:

- "Don't befriend angry people or associate with hot-tempered people" (Proverbs 22:24 NLT).

- "Oh, the joys of those who do not follow the advice of the wicked, or stand around with sinners, or join in with mockers. But they delight in the law of the LORD, meditating on it day and night" (Psalm 1:1–2 NLT).
- "I urge you, brothers and sisters, to watch out for those who cause divisions and put obstacles in your way that are contrary to the teaching you have learned. Keep away from them" (Romans 16:17 NIV).

If you already have godly friendships, treat them like the treasures they are. Give God thanks for them, and express gratitude often. Refuse to take them for granted, respecting their time, boundaries, and opinions.

Look for friends who love the Lord. Look for people who will encourage you in your commitment to Christ. And be that friend who will encourage others in the things of the Lord as well. Remember Proverbs 27:17, which says, "As iron sharpens iron, so a friend sharpens a friend" (NLT).

Prayer: Lord, Thank You for showing us what true friendship is all about. By Your sacrifice, You have displayed the kind of love that sticks closer than a brother. Help me find philia friendships, friends who build up instead of tear down, friends who speak truth instead of flattery, and friends who are sacrificial and not selfish. I will look to Your Word as my guide, not only in seeking wise friends, but in being a godly friend in return. In Jesus' name, amen.

QUESTIONS for Discussion

1. First Corinthians 15:33 says, "Bad company corrupts good character" (NLT). Reflect on how you have been negatively influenced by certain friends. What are some telltale signs that they are "bad company"?

2. Paul gave specific instructions in 2 Timothy 2:22, saying, "Run from anything that stimulates youthful lusts. Instead, pursue righteous living, faithfulness, love, and peace. Enjoy the companionship of those who call on the Lord with pure hearts" (NLT). Are there any current relationships you should prayerfully consider in light of this passage? What might God be calling you to do to protect your heart from negative influences?

3. Proverbs 18:24 distinguishes between destructive friends and real friends, saying, "There are 'friends' who destroy each other, but a real friend sticks closer than a brother" (NLT). Can you think of a few real-life examples of friends who've destroyed each other (through gossip, betrayal, etc.)? In contrast, what are the characteristics of friends who stick closer than a brother?

4. David and Jonathan had deep love for each other—a *philia* kind of love. Can you recount one or two friendships that have displayed *philia* love in your life? How does this type of commitment differ from surface-level friendships or acquaintances?

5. Jonathan was a good example of Philippians 2:3, which says, "Let nothing be done through selfish ambition or conceit, but in lowliness of mind let each esteem others better than himself" (NKJV). In your current relationships, how are you emulating Jonathan's example? What challenges do you face in esteeming others above yourself?

6. This chapter states, "Despite the easy road, the one promising a secure future, Jonathan chose the will of God. In fact, he went in the opposite direction of his father, Saul, which was rather risky." Have you ever chosen the difficult road, knowing it was the right thing to do? What did you give up in order to submit to God's will? In what ways did God bless your obedience?

7. Time and again, the Bible teaches us to be countercultural. The Sermon on the Mount is a great example of this teaching. Reflect on Matthew 5:1–12 and how important it is to be countercultural today. Give practical examples of how to "live in the world but not be part of it." In your friendships, what might be required of you to swim upstream instead of going with the flow?

8. This chapter said, "The best advice from a friend directs our attention to what God has done and will do." What is some of the best advice you've ever received from a friend? How did it redirect your attention to the Lord? In what ways can you faithfully point your friends to Jesus?

9. Proverbs 27:6 says, "Wounds from a sincere friend are better than many kisses from an enemy" (NLT). How can you tell the difference between a sincere friend and a "frenemy" who will tear you down behind your back? From what was shared in this chapter, what are some key indicators of friends you can trust?

10. Jesus said, "Greater love hath no man than this, that a man lay down his life for his friends" (John 15:13 KJV). Apart from Jesus' sacrificial love on the cross, have you ever known someone willing to lay down their life for others? Reflecting on the story of Mikey Monsoor, the Navy Seal, how does his example inspire you to consider your friends' lives over your own?

11. The chapter ends with the encouragement to treat godly friendships "like the treasures they are." In what ways can you nurture true friendships in both words and actions? Think of one friend you can reach out to this week.

CHAPTER 10

Weathering the Storms Together

"In his kindness God called you to share in his eternal glory by means of Christ Jesus. So after you have suffered a little while, he will restore, support, and strengthen you, and he will place you on a firm foundation."
—1 Peter 5:10 (NLT)

Every person, marriage, and family will, at some point, come under attack. Without exception, all of us will weather some serious storms. It won't, however, be the severity of the storms that determine which households survive, but rather the strength of their foundations.

As shared previously, Jesus told this story about two different people who built on two different foundations:

> Anyone who listens to my teaching and follows it is wise, like a person who builds a house on solid rock. Though the rain comes in torrents and the floodwaters rise and the winds beat against that house, it won't collapse because it is built on bedrock. But anyone who hears my teaching and doesn't obey it is foolish, like a person who builds a house on sand. When the rains and floods come and the winds beat against that house, it will collapse with a mighty crash. (Matthew 7:24–27 NLT)

With this in mind, let me ask: Is your marriage built on the Rock or is it on the rocks? If you have built your relationship on Christ the Rock, and the timeless counsel of God's Word, your marriage will withstand those inevitable tests and storms of life.

Our marriage weathered the worst storm ever several years ago, when our 33-year-old son, Christopher, suddenly left for Heaven after a car crash. It broke my heart to see my wife trying to cope with this terrible, devastating event. Cathe loved Christopher, and had a very close relationship with him. It was difficult enough for me to deal with my own pain, but it was that much more agonizing to see my wife plunged into grief and mourning.

Through it all, however, I have seen qualities in Cathe's life that just blow my mind. I always knew she was a woman of God; she is Proverbs 31 right down the line, but since our son's death, I have seen her amazing qualities come to life like never before. And I wouldn't say that if I didn't mean it. She has been a tremendous example to me, through all the days of grief and healing.

Sometimes I wonder (if only for a minute), what it would be like if we didn't have the Lord. What if we didn't have the hope of reunion with Christopher in Heaven? How could we have ever dealt with this? How could we have survived? Even with the Lord, it's been very difficult. But through it all, our marriage has grown stronger than ever before. Why? Because it is built on the Rock, and God has strengthened us through the storm.

When We Lose Our Bearings

Jonathan's Story: I think we all have an idea of what thick fog and storms look like. It reminds me of when I was in high school and went surfing with some friends just south of the Huntington Beach Pier. The fog was so thick, and we knew there was a swell (a series of big waves).

We knew from the forecast that the swell was going to be big, but it was so foggy, we couldn't see the waves at all. We were standing on the shoreline, trying to see how big it was, figuring out our equipment and everything, but all we could hear were the waves crashing. We couldn't even see people in the water. "Okay," we thought. "This is no big deal."

Once we got our equipment, we paddled out, and made our way to what we thought was the lineup. Thankfully, we didn't have to punch through very many waves and got there pretty quickly. But as we were sitting there, we realized that we were not in the lineup; the waves were actually breaking much farther out. We waited until we saw a set come in, and scrambled to get underneath it. And after duck diving 12 waves (at least that's how it felt), I got an ice cream headache from the cold.

Just so you know, when the waves are big in Huntington, there is a serious current like nothing you've experienced before. And it rips from north to south, pushing you south. Basically, if you want to stay in position, you have to constantly be paddling, paddling, paddling.

Now, most people can do this for 30 minutes, or at most, an hour. But after a while, you get tired and let the current take you. So, after being out there as long as I could, I just gave up. My friends and I were split up, (which often happens when you paddle out with friends). And I remember thinking, "I'm just going to let the current take me." Keep in mind, I couldn't see anything. It was extremely foggy, so I just let the current carry me.

Eventually, I caught a final wave in and walked up on shore. Again, it was so foggy, I couldn't see the beach. So, I didn't really know where I was. I walked up to the sand and started looking for some kind of marker, something to get my bearings. I looked up to see Tower 15. I'm like, "Tower 15? That's pretty far!" That's when I started walking north toward the pier . . . walking, and walking, and walking. I had drifted over a mile south from where I first started off.

I'd completely lost my bearings that day, and it reminds me of how, sometimes, we can lose our bearings in marriage. We get caught in the fog of our circumstances or emotions and drift away from our spouse.

Even soldiers talk about being in the fog of war. Oftentimes, they'll land with an objective, but then so many things are happening, their heads start to spin, and they lose sight of what they're supposed to do. They sometimes get separated from the rest of their platoon, and they're unable to complete their objective. They call this "the fog of war."

How often do we lose sight of our objective in marriage: to honor God and our spouse, and to love them through every storm? We let the fog come between us, separating us until we drift so far apart that it's difficult to make our way back together.

Are You Drifting or Anchored?

Through every fog and every storm, Jesus is the anchor for the soul. (Jonathan definitely could have used a literal anchor that day at the Huntington Beach Pier.) But I love that picture of Jesus being the anchor for our soul. He is something we can hold on to, the One who will keep us in place and keep us from drifting.

I think we all know what it's like to spiritually drift. We fall away. We lose sight of what we're supposed to be doing. We don't know what is coming next. We don't know what's going to happen. We don't know what's going on, or who's really in control. We need an anchor.

Think about what we see on the news: corruption, assassinations, exploitation, and so many other terrible things. It can feel like your head is spinning while you try to figure out what is really going on (just like the fog of war).

But everybody wants clarity, right? Everybody wants to know what is coming next. Whether you're single, dating, or married, you want to know what is up ahead. Well, fortunately for us as believers, we have a spiritual compass that always points true north and can direct us through every storm. In the uncertainty, chaos, and confusion, our heavenly Father provides everything we need through His Word.

Getting an Earful

We try to live out the principles that God has given us in His Word, but do we live them out perfectly? No. And I'm the first to admit that. But we're always working at it, applying ourselves. Really, that's the key right there.

We work at it. We cry out to God for His strength and wisdom. And if you do the same, your marriage will weather every storm no matter what.

Sadly, our contemporary culture has plenty to say in opposition of this, and much of it is mocking, cynical, negative, or downright hostile. In the 1950s and '60s, television programs like *Leave It to Beaver, Ozzie and Harriet, Father Knows Best,* and a host of other nightly offerings held up secure, traditional marriages and happy families as models to emulate.

Not any longer.

For years now, faithful husbands and wives, dedicated dads, devoted mothers, and secure, happy kids have been minimized, discounted, parodied, and ridiculed. Movies glorify the "adventure" of adulterous relationships, and portray men and women who choose to remain virgins until marriage as strange, eccentric people who are only to be pitied.

Yes, we certainly get an eyeful and earful from the world around us, about dating, marriage, and divorce. But I hope you're not looking to celebrity culture for your cues on how to have a successful marriage. You won't get any helpful or lasting information from the tabloids.

The Bible, however, has a great deal to say on the subject, and its information is as relevant today as it was two thousand years ago.

Challenging the Assumptions

In His Sermon on the Mount, Jesus challenged some old and deeply held assumptions—to the amazement of His listeners.

Beginning with the phrase "you have heard that it was said" (NIV), He took on one traditionally held opinion after another, contrasting those teachings with God's actual intent. By the time He came to the subject of marriage, divorce, and adultery, He must have had everyone's almost breathless attention.

> It has been said, "Whoever divorces his wife, let him give her a certificate of divorce." But I say to you that whoever divorces

his wife for any reason except sexual immorality causes her to commit adultery; and whoever marries a woman who is divorced commits adultery. (Matthew 5:31–32 NKJV)

Sometime later, He had occasion to add to those remarks.

> The Pharisees also came to Him, testing Him, and saying to Him, "Is it lawful for a man to divorce his wife for just any reason?"
>
> And He answered and said to them, "Have you not read that He who made them at the beginning 'made them male and female,' and said, 'For this reason a man shall leave his father and mother and be joined to his wife, and the two shall become one flesh'? So then, they are no longer two but one flesh. Therefore what God has joined together, let not man separate." (Matthew 19:3–6 NKJV)

It's interesting how Jesus immediately answers the Pharisees' question by flashing back to the beginning of time and the creation of Adam and Eve. And why not? He was there! No one could know better how God had intended the husband-wife relationship to work than the One who invented it in the first place.

Reflecting on God's design for marriage, commentator Matthew Henry wrote, "Eve was made by God, not out of [Adam's] head to rule over him, nor out of his feet to be trampled upon by him, but out of his side, to be equal with him. Under his arm to be protected, and near his heart to be loved."[17]

When you think about it, Adam and Eve had everything you would want for an ideal marriage. She would never have to hear about the way his mother cooked, and he didn't have to hear about all of the other men she could have married!

So, that's the way Jesus chose to open the subject. Before He spoke about the tragedy of divorce, He first walked the Pharisees back to a beautiful garden at the beginning of time, to a man and woman who lived together and loved one another without so much as a shadow of conflict.

Jesus wasn't afraid to challenge any assumptions, and we shouldn't be either.

The Seismic Destruction of Divorce

Wedlock is to be a padlock; it is to be a lock, and you throw away the key. Divorce cannot be an option the moment you say "I do." However, I would venture to say that everyone reading these words has been impacted by divorce in some way.

Perhaps you've experienced this heartache personally. Or maybe it was your parents, grown children, or close friends who went through divorce. You've seen it up close, and in some way, shape, or form, it has cast its long shadow across your life. Certainly, divorce is on the rise in our culture and has been for many years.

According to statistics, there is now one divorce for every 1.8 marriages.[18] Over a million children per year are involved in divorce, and without question, it is wreaking havoc on our country. As Pope John Paul II well said, "As the family goes, so goes the nation."[19]

Through the years, I have noted that most of our nation's ills can be directly traced to the breakdown of the family. If ever there was a time that we needed to do everything we could to keep our marriages together, the time is now.

It seems to me that people will dissolve their marriages over practically anything these days. They say to themselves:

> *This is just too hard.*

> *I'll end this marriage and slide into a new relationship.*

> *It will be a new beginning for me, and I'll leave all my problems and heartaches behind.*

What people discover, however, is that their problems follow right behind them into the new relationship, and they end up being every bit as unhappy as before—or even more so. When it comes to divorce, there is no such thing as a "clean break." Divorce is very, very messy, and it always will be.

In the book *Second Chances*, psychologist and researcher Judith Wallerstein wrote, "Divorce can be deceptive. Legally, it's a single event, but psychologically it's a chain. Sometimes a never-ending chain of events, relocations, and radically shifting relationships strung through time, a process that forever changes the lives of the people involved."[20]

There is no doubt divorce wreaks havoc and causes widespread destruction. It's a storm of tremendous size that moves slowly through families, leaving everyone to pick up the pieces.

Irreconcilable Differences Don't Count

Yes, there are biblical grounds for divorce, but the number one reason couples cite for ending their marriage is "irreconcilable differences."

As I've said many times before, this phrase drives me absolutely crazy. Irreconcilable differences? Everybody has irreconcilable differences. My wife and I have had them for over 50 years. She's very neat; I'm often messy. She tends to be late; I'm usually early. She likes the toilet seat down; I like it up. (I'm still working on that one. Even my granddaughter scolds me, "Papa, put the toilet seat down!")

Some of the very qualities that attracted you to your mate in the beginning somehow morph into issues that divide you. Why did you like this person in the first place? Because he or she was different than you! She was outgoing and talkative; you were quiet and reserved. He was creative and impulsive; you were practical and cautious.

And now it's driving you crazy? Now it's an "irreconcilable difference"? Give me a break! Why can't these differences—*any* differences—be resolved in the strength and grace of Jesus Christ? Sometimes you just have to take a deep breath, square your shoulders, and say, "This thing may never change, but I made a vow to stand by my mate for richer or for poorer, for better or for worse, in sickness and in health. I'm going to love him anyway. I'm going to stick with her through it all."

Here's the truth of the matter: The Bible doesn't recognize "irreconcilable differences" as a reason to dissolve a marriage. Did you hear that? I know it goes against what the culture heavily promotes, but it is not biblical.

In Jesus' day, there was a very lax attitude toward marriage. The divorce laws were heavily weighted in favor of men, and a man could divorce his wife for pretty much any reason.

According to one rabbi of the day, you could send your wife away for "incompatibility of temperament." (Which sounds a lot like "irreconcilable differences" to me.) A man could also divorce his wife for such trivial things as burning his meal, embarrassing him in front of his friends, or letting her hair down in public. And according to the rabbi known as Akiba, a man could send his wife away simply because another, more attractive woman came along.[21]

How absurd. Yet this was the prevalent attitude in the day when the Pharisees posed their question to Christ: "Why then did Moses command that a man give his wife a certificate of divorce and send her away?" (Matthew 19:7 NKJV).

Jesus answered them, but changed a key term. He said, "Moses, because of the hardness of your hearts, permitted you to divorce your wives" (verse 8 NKJV).

They said *commanded*. Jesus said *permitted*.

Moses didn't "command" any man to divorce his wife. But because of the hardness and callousness of man's heart, Moses permitted what amounts to a release clause for the sake of the woman. This provision in the law allowed her to escape from the hardship of trying to carry on in a home where she was unloved and unwanted, all because a man had failed to live up to the high ideal of marriage.

So, when is divorce allowed?

Divorce Is Allowed when Sexual Immorality Takes Place

Matthew 19:9 says, "I say to you, whoever divorces his wife, except for sexual immorality, and marries another, commits adultery" (NKJV).

Back in the Sermon on the Mount text, Jesus said in Matthew 5:32, "Whoever divorces his wife for any reason except sexual immorality causes her to commit adultery" (NKJV).

Okay, but what is sexual immorality? The biblical term comes from the Greek *pornea*. (We get the word *pornography* from this word.) It speaks of extramarital sexual relations, including the so-called "affair." This includes any sex outside of marriage, including incest, prostitution, and homosexuality.

Why is immorality a potential deal-breaker in a marriage? Because the oneness of the marriage bond has been violated. Paul even said, "Do you not know that he who unites himself with a prostitute is one with her in body?" (1 Corinthians 6:16 NIV).

Yes, you could call it a "one-night stand" or a "fling." You could say it didn't really mean anything.

But it means a lot to God, and it should mean a lot to you. When you have sex with someone besides your spouse, you enter into a union with that person, and violate the union between you and your mate. Adultery is pure poison. Adultery wounds, scars, withers, kills, and tears into the fabric of a marriage and a home like nothing else. Our 21st-century culture—with its books, magazines, movies and celebrities—seems to work overtime to make adultery seem trivial, natural, no-big-deal, and even to be expected.

But it's all a lie. It's like whitewashing a tomb full of rotting bones. As the book of Proverbs says, "Adultery is a brainless act, soul-destroying, self-destructive" (6:32 MSG).

What the world calls an "affair" or an "indiscretion" is, in reality, a sin that will wound you and others to the very core, and will affect you for the rest of your life. If you're still not convinced, here are six reasons to *not* commit adultery:

1. Adultery does incredible damage to your spouse
In 1 Corinthians 6:16, the apostle Paul writes: "He who unites himself with a prostitute is one with her in body" (NIV).

When you committed your life to your wife or husband, the two of you became one flesh. But if you have sex with someone else, you violate that oneness with your spouse and enter into a oneness with that other person.

But you insist, "It's only a one-night stand." Don't deceive yourself. There is no such thing.

Even though Jesus gave a release clause from the marriage because of the seriousness of this offense, it is *not* to say that if you have been unfaithful to your spouse they should divorce you, or vice versa. Listen, adultery is not only grounds for divorce, but it is also grounds for forgiveness. I encourage you to forgive your spouse and give them another chance.

2. *Adultery does incredible damage to yourself*

To even get to the place where you're willing to commit adultery means you've had to harden yourself against God. In essence, you've already been living in a backslidden state that is hurting you spiritually. Not only that, but you have also put yourself at great risk physically. Sexually transmitted diseases (STDs) are potential problems with anyone who is sexually immoral in this culture.

One of the biggest myths that has been propagated by our culture—especially among our nation's youth—is the concept of "safe sex." It's a blatant lie. I could cite statistic after statistic about how it *isn't safe,* and how there is a great risk factor involved.

A few years ago, I spoke with an individual who had come to our church for counseling. He was terrified because he had been unfaithful to his wife on many occasions and thought he had an STD. He had been tested and was waiting for the results. He had to go home and tell his wife what he had done. He had put himself and his marriage at risk while he was out fooling around. What a tragedy.

If you haven't noticed, people don't think clearly when they are hooked by lust and sexual sin. It's as if a fog descends over their brains. That's why the Bible warns us to stay away from it, because of its deceptive allure and the power it can exercise over our minds.

It reminds me of a news story I read about a man who lived in England. He had a pet scorpion, which he named Twiggy. Apparently, each night this man would take Twiggy in his hand and give him a little kiss goodnight. One night, to his total surprise, the scorpion stung him on the lip. When the man opened his mouth in shock, the scorpion jumped in and stung him again.

Two things came to mind when I read that story. I won't tell you what the first thing was, because it wouldn't be kind. But the second thing I thought of was that this man underestimated the nature of that creature.

In the same way, we will commit (in our estimation) a "little" sin—something that we don't think is significant. Then we're shocked when it turns around and bites us. We're shocked when it hurts us. We can't believe it happened.

The fact is that no one who is daily walking with Jesus Christ suddenly "falls" into adultery. It's not like some deep pothole in the road that catches you unaware; it's more a cliff-edge that a person keeps straying closer and closer to. Adultery occurs after much denial, self-deception, and rationalization. And once you commit adultery, there is vulnerability in your life. The enemy will continue to attack you in this area. You have crossed a line that cannot be uncrossed.

In other words, it's easier to commit adultery a second time when you have done it a first time. It's a bit like breaking a limb. I broke my wrist years ago, and to this day I still feel a weakness there. If I'm not careful, I could break it again. In the same way, there is vulnerability in the life of someone who has already yielded to this devastating sin.

You might say, "Wait a second. Won't God forgive me?"

Sure, He will. But others won't forgive you as quickly. Some never will. And radical measures must be taken to prevent this from ever happening again.

You say, "Well, I'll just marry the person I had the fling with."

Really? But what kind of foundation for marriage would that be? Would you be able to trust a person who has already been unfaithful? Would he or she be able to trust you? Talk about getting off on the wrong foot!

Adultery does incredible damage to a person, no matter how you look at it. You can paint a harmless picture of it, but like Twiggy the pet scorpion, it will eventually come back to bite you.

3. *Adultery does incredible damage to your children*

If you break your marriage vows, your position as spiritual leader in your home will be undermined by your own hand. The trust and respect your children had for you will be as eroded as it is with your spouse. What's worse, your children might even follow in your footsteps and repeat your sin in their own lives.

I remember hearing the story of a man who had committed adultery, and his young daughter found out about it. As she grew into a young woman, she started living in a promiscuous way, and he confronted her.

"Honey," he said. "You can't do this. You can't live like this."

"Why not?" she replied. "You did."

And what could he reply to that?

Even a spiritual giant like King David had to watch as some of his children repeated his sins of adultery, deception, and murder. God forgave David, yes, but David still had to reap the consequences of his rebellion and sin for the rest of his life.

We don't live to ourselves, and we don't die to ourselves. Our decisions in this life—even if we repent of them and find forgiveness—can impact our descendants for generations to come.

4. *Adultery does incredible damage to the church*

The Scripture teaches that when one member of the body of Christ suffers, we all suffer. When one of us is exalted or God uses one of us in a unique or effective way, we are all blessed. And by the same token, when one of us falls into sin, it touches all of us.

If you are a child of God, you no longer live unto yourself. You don't live on an island. As a result, your actions truly do affect the church as a whole. That is why Paul exhorted the believers in Corinth to remove an immoral man from their midst, because "a little yeast leavens the whole batch of dough" (1 Corinthians 5:6 NIV).

Even one immoral person who has seriously compromised God's command, and continues to hide his or her sin, will have a poisonous, paralyzing impact on the effectiveness of the local church.

5. *Adultery does incredible damage to the cause of Christ*

When people in the church or in ministry commit adultery, it does incredible damage to the cause of Christ. When unbelievers find out, they become even more cynical of Christians. And even believers can become discouraged in their faith.

The prophet Nathan warned David of this after the king had fallen into sin and then covered it up. Nathan said, "By this deed you have given great occasion to the enemies of the LORD to blaspheme" (2 Samuel 12:14 NKJV).

Adultery provides occasion for the enemies of Christ to point fingers and discount our witness. What a tragedy!

6. *Adultery is a sin against the Lord*

This should be the primary reason we would want to avoid this sin—but often it's the last thing we think about. Adultery is sin against the Lord, against the Savior who loves you. When you forsake your marriage vows, you sin against the One who purchased you with His own blood. You drag His name through the mud. Doesn't that matter to you?

I think what is lacking in the hearts of many Christians today is the fear of God. By "the fear of God," I don't mean the fear of righteous retribution, but the fear of displeasing Him. One of the best definitions I've heard of the fear of God is "a wholesome dread of displeasing Him." In other words, you love God so much that you don't want to do something that would displease Him and bring shame to His name and to the cause of His kingdom.

Having said all that, however, you don't have to get a divorce if immorality has taken place. In fact, I would even say that every effort should be made to restore the marriage. Both partners should examine the steps that led to this sin, and apply some preventative measures. But by all means, try to save the marriage.

If you only hear one thing about adultery, let it be that it is grievous and displeasing to the Lord. And isn't that enough?

Divorce Is Allowed when Desertion Takes Place

In 1 Corinthians 7:13, Paul says that "if a woman has a husband who is not a believer and he is willing to live with her, she must not divorce him" (NIV).

So, we have a Christian who has been united in marriage to a non-Christian. How does this happen? It happens because of disobedience. It happens in spite of the Bible's clear warning against an "equal yoke" in marriage (2 Corinthians 6:14).

A Christian will become impatient waiting to find that right guy or that right girl, and will marry the first person who becomes available. Then, as time goes by, the believer invariably realizes he or she should never have done that, and sometimes they start looking for the back door.

Again, here is what Scripture tells us: "If a woman has a husband who is not a believer and he is willing to live with her, she must not divorce him" (1 Corinthians 7:13 NIV).

Your job description now, Christian woman, is to win that man to Christ.

The passage goes on to say:

> "For perhaps the husband who isn't a Christian may become a Christian with the help of his Christian wife. And the wife who isn't a Christian may become a Christian with the help of her Christian husband. Otherwise, if the family separates, the children might never come to know the Lord; whereas a united family may, in God's plan, result in the children's salvation" (1 Corinthians 7:14 TLB).

But let's say the nonbeliever departs—he or she abandons you. Paul goes on to say in 1 Corinthians 7 that in such cases, a brother or a sister is not "bound," because God has called us to peace. The phrase used there for "bound" means "held by consent of agreement, or to be a slave of." So, if the nonbeliever leaves, you are free.

But what if he or she claims to be a Christian? It doesn't matter. It's the leaving that matters, not whether the departing partner claims to know Jesus. Quite frankly, if any man or woman would leave their spouse—claiming the leading of the Lord—when that spouse wants them to stay, I would have to question if that person was a Christian at all.

The Bible says, "Anyone who does not provide for their relatives, and especially for their on household, has denied the faith and is worse than an unbeliever" (1 Timothy 5:8 NIV).

The proof of our faith is not just in what we say, it is in what we *do*. So, if your spouse abandons you, if he or she leaves you, according to Scripture you are not held to the agreement any longer.

Keep Trying at All Costs

I cannot emphasize enough the importance of trying to keep your marriage together at all costs. Couples give up far too quickly, especially when they're offended. But let's be clear about the utter devastation that divorce brings.

In a book titled *The Divorce Revolution*, the author made this statement: "Divorce and separated people have the highest admission rates to psychiatric facilities. It takes its toll on the physical well-being of the people. Divorced people have more illness, higher mortality rates, and higher suicide rates."[22]

And that's not even to mention the children.

Some time ago, a *Newsweek* article noted:

> The emotional wounds [of the children of divorce] run deep—and time does not always heal. Divorce remains a central issue throughout their lives no matter how well adjusted they may seem. A hole in the heart is universal.... There is a sense of having missed out on something that is a birthright, the right to grow up in a house with two parents.
>
> Compared with people who have grown up with intact families, adult children of divorce are more likely to have troubled relationships, broken marriages. A desire for stability sends some down

the aisle at too young an age and they end up in divorce court not long afterward.[23]

So much for that despicable fiction about children of divorce being "resilient." It's a lie perpetuated to make the one getting a divorce feel better about their decisions.

But here's the bottom line: Divorces that have a legitimate basis in Scripture are *extremely rare*. Trust me on this one. Throughout all my years of ministry, most divorces I have seen could have been avoided if the husband and wife would have humbled themselves and simply begun obeying the Word of God.

That's where it all begins: with a commitment to obey God. It continues with an ongoing commitment to daily (and even hourly) trust God, drawing on His life, wisdom, joy, and power, even when times are very, *very* tough.

Can we say that we will submit ourselves and our marriage to what the Word of God says? Can we commit to trying to do this God's way, instead of the world's way? With God's help, periodically take stock of your marriage and see if there's anything that might be bringing division between you and your spouse. If you identify it, whatever it is, get rid of it. Your goal is to keep trying at all costs.

Prepare and Protect

Weathering the storms that come—those great, dark storms that you can almost track as they roll over the horizon—often depends on how well you've prepared. And for those sudden, unexpected storms that rip through your life like a flash flood? Or the temptations and attacks that come uninvited? You'd better do what you can now to protect your home from the perils that will surely come.

A few years ago, Southern California faced terrible firestorms fanned by the relentless Santa Ana winds. I remember reading about one man's home in a wooded area that had somehow survived a fire that destroyed the homes in his neighborhood. The newspaper showed a huge photo of a blackened, devastated area, with this man's home—gleaming, white, and seemingly untouched—in the midst of it.

They asked this man, "What's your secret?"

"I just went above code for building," he replied. "I sealed the eaves. I used double-paned glass. I went above and beyond the requirements of everything they said." So, when the fire came, it didn't burn his house.

In the same way, we need to do what we can to defend our lives, homes, marriages, and families against the fires of Hell that would like to burn them to the ground.

It takes some extra caution and extra preparation. It means going the extra mile, and refusing to "just get by" with the bare minimum. It means giving it your all and working as a team. It means determining in your heart that your wife or your husband will be your best friend and confidant through every trial.

As you do your part to shore up your home, it will still be standing when the flames roar overhead and torch other homes and marriages all around you. And you know what? The effort will be worth it. A million times over.

Building the Boat to Weather Every Storm

We've talked in depth about weathering storms in marriage, from the loss of a child to unfaithfulness and divorce. Truly, these are difficult waves to manage, and they can easily pull us under if we're not careful. But let's take a look at a familiar story in the Bible, the story of Noah.

Starting with the most powerful verse in this story, Genesis 6:22 says, "Noah did everything just as God commanded him" (NIV). The New Living Translation says it this way: "So Noah did everything *exactly* as God had commanded him" (emphasis mine).

Just in case you forgot what happened, when Noah was 600 years old, all the underground waters erupted from the earth, and the rain fell in mighty torrents from the sky. The rain continued to fall for 40 days and 40 nights. The first day, Noah had gone into the boat with his wife and sons, Shem, Ham, and Japheth, along with their wives. With them in the boat were pairs of every kind of animal, domestic and wild, large and small, along with birds of every kind.

Genesis 7:17–18 tells us, "For forty days the floodwaters grew deeper, covering the ground and lifting the boat high above the earth. As the waters rose higher and higher above the ground, the boat floated safely on the surface" (NLT). And in the latter part of verse 23, we read, "The only people who survived were Noah and those with him in the boat. And the floodwaters covered the earth for 150 days" (NLT).

I share this story to emphasize the importance of building your "boat" according to God's design. And to build it, you're going to need to follow God's *exact* blueprint. Do everything He commands. Follow His instructions.

Isn't this what we've been saying all along?

Listen to God's voice over the noise of the culture.

Do what He says, even when it doesn't make sense to the world.

Build on the solid foundation of Jesus Christ, your anchor in times of storm.

It's the only way, my friend.

Prayer: Lord, our spirit is willing, but our flesh is weak. So, Father, we ask You for a fresh outpouring of Your Holy Spirit upon us. We know we're not perfect; we know we fall short. But You are faithful, Lord, even when we are faithless. You are always there to pick us up. Please strengthen us to weather every storm. Help us navigate thick fog and darkness with the light of Your Word. Unite us as one, Lord, the way You designed our marriages. In sorrow, grief, betrayal, and feelings of defeat, remind us that You are our strong anchor. We can weather any storm by the power of Your Spirit. So, show us grace, Lord; we need Your grace each and every day of our lives. Help us build our lives and our marriages through integrity, character, and nearness to You. In Jesus' name, amen.

QUESTIONS for Discussion

1. It was said in this chapter, "It won't, however, be the severity of the storms that determine which households survive, but rather the

strength of their foundations." How does Matthew 7:24–27 enforce this statement?

2. Jonathan shared a surfing story about drifting through the fog and ending up more than a mile from where he started. How does this relate to marriage when couples drift apart in the fog of their circumstances or emotions? What are some ways you can prevent drifting in your marriage?

3. This chapter says, "Everybody wants clarity, right? Everybody wants to know what is coming next." How does Jesus, our True North, give us clarity through life's storms? What are the blessings of relying on God's compass instead of the culture's?

4. Greg emphasized how Jesus challenged assumptions and how we should too. What are some of the world's assumptions about divorce, and how does God's view contrast these? Are there any assumptions you've made that need to come into alignment with the Bible?

5. Greg wrote, "Through the years I have noted that most of our nation's ills can be directly traced to the breakdown of the family. If ever there was a time we needed to do everything we could to keep our marriages together, the time is now." If our nation's ills can indeed be traced back to the systematic destruction of our marriages and families, what positive impact can even one intact, happy, God-centered marriage have on an apartment complex . . . a block . . . a neighborhood . . . or a city?

6. Sometimes, people contemplating divorce imagine that ending their marriage will be a quick escape or fresh new beginning to life. What factors are they failing to take into consideration?

7. Greg challenges the notion of so-called "irreconcilable differences" and cites how very different he is from his wife in so many ways. The fact is that any difference can be reconciled in the strength and grace of Jesus Christ. Describe the mindset and commitment necessary in a marriage to face up to differences and "work things out" with the help of Almighty God.

8. Greg reflected, "Some of the very qualities that attracted you to your mate in the beginning somehow morph into issues that divide you. Why did you like this person in the first place? Because he or she was different than you!" Think of the differences between you and your spouse that once attracted you, and now annoy you. What has changed? Have those differences become more pronounced, or have you become less patient and more self-centered?

9. Why is immorality a potential deal-breaker in a marriage? And do such sins mean that divorce is inevitable? What are some possible advantages of working through the pain, anger, and heartbreak of marital infidelity in order to preserve a marriage?

10. According to 1 Corinthians 7:13–14, what is the opportunity and "job description" of a Christian spouse who is married to a non-Christian husband or wife?

11. There was the story of a man who lived in a densely wooded neighborhood and went the extra mile to protect his home in the event of a forest fire. He succeeded by going beyond the suggested building codes and taking more precautions than anyone required or expected. As a result, his home was left standing when the rest of the neighborhood went up in flames. How can you bring that same sort of above-and-beyond care, preparation, and precaution to your marriage, the most valuable human relationship of your life?

12. It was said in this chapter, "To even get to the place where you're willing to commit adultery means you've had to harden yourself against God. In essence, you've already been living in a backslidden state that is hurting you spiritually." Read Hebrews 3:12–13, and then answer this question: Why is it important for believers to encourage one another daily to walk with God and turn away from sin? According to these verses, what might happen to the one who withdraws from the exhortation and encouragement of fellow believers?

13. Christians who choose to engage in immorality sometimes feel like they are only hurting themselves. Paul, however, exhorted the believers in Corinth to remove an immoral man from their midst, because

"a little yeast leavens the whole batch of dough" (1 Corinthians 5:6 NIV). What did Paul mean by that? How does the sin of one member of Christ's body affect the whole?

14. This chapter closed with Genesis 6:22, which says, "Noah did everything exactly as God had commanded him" (NLT). In what ways does following God's exact blueprint help you weather storms? On a personal level? As a married couple? As a parent?

CHAPTER 11

Passing On the Legacy

*"You and your children and grandchildren must fear the L*ORD *your God as long as you live. If you obey all his decrees and commands, you will enjoy a long life."*—Deuteronomy 6:2 (NLT)

There are telltale signs that you are getting old. That little gray-haired lady you are helping across the street is your wife. Your little black book only contains names ending in M.D. You dim the lights for economic reasons, not romantic ones. Your back goes out more than you do. And you notice that your children are starting to look middle-aged.

But long before this stage of life, we should be thinking about what we are leaving behind. Are we living a life that is worth emulating? What kind of legacy will we leave for the next generation?

When David was on his deathbed, he called in his son Solomon. Solomon was going to carry on his reign as king. Here is what David said to him: "As for you, my son Solomon, know the God of your father, and serve Him with a loyal heart and with a willing mind; for the LORD searches all hearts and understands all the intent of the thoughts. If you seek Him, He will be found by you; but if you forsake Him, He will cast you off forever" (1 Chronicles 28:9 NKJV).

Like David, we are all leaving a legacy. And our job as parents is to bring our children to Christ, by our actions and by our words. The legacy we leave for those who follow will affect generations to come.

From all that we've covered in this book, our number one relationship goal is to glorify God in all that we say and do. Passing on a strong example of a life lived for Christ is one of the most important things we could ever do in our personal walks, our marriages, our families, and our careers. Every area submitted to God's plan is a testimony to His good, pleasing, and perfect will. Amen?

Keeping Our Eyes on Jesus (The Eye of the Tiger)

I remember when our granddaughter Allie was a little girl playing soccer. She was on a team called the Purple Princesses. Well, she wasn't scoring any goals, so I said, "Allie, you need the eye of the tiger." She looked at me quizzically, indicating she'd never seen *Rocky III,* so I said, "Okay, I'll tell you what. I'll give you a doll if you score a goal." Well, wouldn't you know, she got the eye of the tiger real quick, and started scoring goal after goal. Finally, I said, "Okay, okay. The doll deal is over. You're scoring too many goals."

But here's my point: Don't lose the eye of the tiger. Scripture tells us that we are to "run with perseverance the race marked out for us" (Hebrews 12:1 NIV).

And how do we do this? We keep our eyes on Jesus.

Hebrews 12 goes on to say that we're all running a race. The writer tells us to lay aside every weight and the sin that so easily besets us or slows us down. He says to run this race with endurance, and here's the key: "Looking unto Jesus, the author and finisher of our faith, who for the joy that was set before Him endured the cross, despising the shame, and has sat down at the right hand of God" (Hebrews 12:2 NKJV).

So, the key is looking to Jesus, keeping your eyes on the Lord, because the devil wants you to take your eyes off of the Lord. He wants you to give up. In fact, the devil's two favorite words are "give up." But don't listen to him! As James 4:7 says, "Resist the devil and he will flee from you" (NKJV).

Perhaps I'm talking to someone right now who is thinking of giving up— giving up on your marriage, your family, your faith, or even your life. If this is you, please be encouraged today. Don't give up, *get up*. Get up and fix your eyes on Jesus. Recall Nehemiah 4:14, which says, "Don't be afraid of the enemy! Remember the Lord" (NLT).

Passing on your legacy starts with keeping your eyes on Jesus, the author and perfecter of your faith. He helps you. He encourages you. He even prays for you.

So, when our kids see us running our race of faith, imperfect as it may be, they'll receive the legacy of a life lived for the King of kings.

Speaking to Men

Listen, friends, our family is our first responsibility before God and our most important mission field. Our legacy depends on it.

When you die someday, what are you going to leave behind? Your career, money, house, and car? These things mean nothing. But your children and grandchildren are the ones left with your legacy. They are going to represent you, what you stood for, and what you taught them. Let's impart to our children the legacy shown to us by Jesus Christ—the forgiveness He extended, the love He displayed, and the grace He offered.

No matter how many times you've dropped the ball, God is the God of second, third, fourth, and fifth chances, isn't He? We have opportunities *daily* to confess, repent, and start again. In whatever area of marriage, family, or work, we can start again, glorify God, and leave a lasting legacy.

Let me ask this: How much study have you done about leading your children? How many parenting books have you read? How much time have you spent one on one with your children individually, teaching them, loving them, explaining to them who Jesus is and what He's done for them?

Many fathers today are on autopilot, showing no initiative in their families. You show initiative at work, you show initiative with your stock portfolio, you show initiative in your fantasy football team, but you know nothing about what the Bible says concerning raising children in the training and admonition of the Lord.

"Well, that's my wife's responsibility," you might say.

If you showed the same initiative at work that you do with your family right now, would you be getting promoted or fired?

Most dads feel like they're doing their job if they provide food and shelter for their families, right? They think, "If my kids have a warm bed to sleep in, food on the table, and I'm not breaking their arm or something, then you know what? I'm a pretty good dad."

If that's the standard you're setting, then you're on par with a possum, okay? Possums have that same goal in mind; they want to make sure their babies are raised to survive childhood. But is that *really* the bar you want to set for your manhood?

Ephesians 6:4 says, "Fathers, do not provoke your children to anger, but bring them up in the discipline and instruction of the Lord" (ESV).

I can't think of anything more provoking than a father who refuses to invest in their child's emotional well-being and spiritual upbringing, but criticizes and corrects them at every turn. Correction without connection will not produce lasting fruit in our young ones. They need more than that; they need an invested, loving relationship that includes faithful guidance in the things of God.

James Merritt, in his book *What God Wants Every Dad to Know*, wrote, "Fatherhood is more than conceiving, feeding, clothing, educating, and sending children out on their own. Dads have the responsibility of preparing their children for the eternal destiny of meeting God."[24]

I agree with that. We are passing on an eternal legacy, and the choices we make concerning how we invest in our children are binding—not just during life here on earth, but forever.

Encouraging Women

Ladies, I know how important it is for you to build your homes and families on close-knit relationships and strong biblical principles. But the culture could care less about these things. Instead, modern families are being built on the foundation of Little League, the arts, education, or some other worldly success. But when those trials come, and those difficulties happen, many will wish that they had established their homes on the foundation of God and His Word.

I'm here to tell you that children grow best in two soils: the home and the church. Kids will thrive in a home that is centered around Jesus Christ, not Little League. Your home is the place to live out the gospel and demonstrate what God has done for you in a practical and tangible way.

Home is the place to teach your kids who God is. Not just giving them the head knowledge, not just teaching them Bible stories and memory verses (which are great, by the way), but also teaching their hearts by example.

Kids are smart. They are watching you. They are observing how you handle real-life situations. It might not seem like it, but they are listening, and you teach them every day through your words and actions.

Deuteronomy 6:1–2 says,

> "These are the commands, decrees, and regulations that the LORD your God commanded me to teach you. You must obey them in the land you are about to enter and occupy, and you and your children and grandchildren must fear the Lord your God as long as you live. If you obey all his decrees and commands, you will enjoy a long life" (NLT).

As mentioned earlier, family is a father's first responsibility before God, his most important mission field. And a mother's responsibility is just as important. You've got to teach your kids the Word. You've got to teach them Scripture. You've got to teach them the Ten Commandments. You've got to teach them who God is. And, you absolutely must live by example.

Raising Our Children in Community

When we brought our first little baby home, we quickly realized how unprepared we were. We didn't get an orientation, we didn't get a booklet, we didn't get anything. The nurses just sent us on our way saying, "Hey, good luck to you. We'll see you for your next checkup."

No learner's permit, no manual, no emergency button. Nothing. We just had to figure it out. Even though we had read all the books and thought we had a decent handle on what was going to happen, we didn't. What about when they grow up a bit and throw their first tantrum? Or what about when they make direct eye contact with you and push their bowl right off the edge of the highchair? What do you do as a parent then? What are you supposed to do at that point? It's a whole new ballgame.

From the moment you bring that kid home, you as parents are responsible, not only for their physical well-being but also their spiritual upbringing. And it starts by establishing a few things from the start.

Psalm 127 says,

> Unless the LORD builds a house, the work of the builders is wasted. Unless the LORD protects a city, guarding it with sentries will do no good. It is useless for you to work so hard from early morning until late at night, anxiously working for food to eat; for God gives rest to his loved ones. Children are a gift from the LORD; they are a reward from him. Children born to a young man are like arrows in a warrior's hands. How joyful is the man whose quiver is full of them! He will not be put to shame when he confronts his accusers at the city gates. (NLT)

In order for a house, a home, and a family to endure, God has to establish it. Did you hear that? God is the one who establishes your family, and from that foundation, you build it brick by brick, discipling your kids every step of the way.

Listen, you have a house that the Lord has built. You have your family. You have a foundation that is laid upon Jesus. Well done. But your house needs to be part of a village. You and your children need to be part of a community. Your family needs to be part of a city that includes other houses built on the same foundation as yours. "Unless the LORD protects a city, guarding it with sentries will do no good" (Psalm 127:1 NLT).

Where are you going to find that community? Where are you going to find that city of other houses that are built like yours—other families that are built on the foundation of Jesus Christ? The church, right? The church is where you're going to find that city. That's where you're going to find that community.

Believe it or not, your kids need a second family. It can't just be all about mom, dad, and siblings, because you know what? There are certain things parents tell their kids, but when a friend at church or youth worker tells them the exact same thing, it resonates in a whole new way. That's why kids need church. They need mentors besides their parents. This is a huge part of discipleship, and a huge part of a child's legacy.

Growing Together Through Momentum

When you get a new surfboard, speed is the most important thing. It's what you want; you want it to carry momentum. Speed and forward energy are everything.

For those of you who are not surf-inclined, you could think of it as trying to ride a bicycle without moving forward. It really doesn't work. You must have forward-moving speed on a bicycle or else you'll fall over. And the same goes with surfing; if you don't have speed on a surfboard, you fall.

Well, I don't think it's any coincidence that the Bible talks about the same thing—momentum, speed, and endurance—to describe our faith. That's why the apostle Paul, who wrote the majority of the New Testament and planted churches all over the ancient world, had this to say in Philippians 3:14, "I press on toward the goal to win the prize for which God has called me heavenward in Christ Jesus" (NIV).

So, whether you're a brand-new believer or you've been walking with the Lord for 10, 20, or 80 years, you should never arrive at a place where you stop moving forward. There's no coasting in the Christian life because the moment you think that you have arrived, and you can put your feet up and relax, that is the moment your spiritual fall begins to take place. The moment you start drifting, the moment you think you've made it, and the moment you take your foot off that gas pedal, that's when things start to fall apart.

Growing together as a family doesn't mean you'll do everything perfectly. It doesn't mean you won't mess up, won't stumble. But when you stumble, how long are you going to stay down? You should get right back up and keep walking in faith. Keep pursuing that finish line.

To encourage you to keep going, keep growing, Philippians 3:12–16 says,

> I don't mean to say that I have already achieved these things or that I have already reached perfection. But I press on to possess that perfection for which Christ Jesus first possessed me. No, dear brothers and sisters, I have not achieved it, but I focus on this one thing: Forgetting the past and looking forward to what lies ahead, I press on to reach the end of the race and receive the heavenly prize for which God, through Christ Jesus, is calling us. Let all who are spiritually mature agree on these things. If you disagree on some point, I believe God will make it plain to you. But we must hold on to the progress we have already made (NLT).

It's not about reaching perfection on earth but pressing on to our heavenly prize. This is not only for our benefit, but for the benefit of our children, grandchildren, and great-grandchildren. As Paul said, "Let all who are spiritually mature agree on these things."

Weapons of Our Warfare

When everything else lets you down, everything else leaves you empty, and nothing else satisfies or delivers, remember it's your relationship with God through His Son, Jesus Christ, that will transform your life. You can never have enough of Him. You'll always be hungry for more of the peace and contentment only Jesus can give. It's like nothing else this world has to offer.

And so, if that is the goal—to know God, love Him, and glorify Him— what are some strategies we can employ in this life to help us continue with that goal, and pass on the legacy?

At Harvest Crusades, we tell everybody who comes down on the field that there are four things they can do so that they will never write the word *back-slider* after their name. If they follow these four disciplines, it will literally change their life. We call them "the weapons of our warfare" or "RPGS."

Read your Bible

Pray

Go to church

Share your faith

A friend of Jonathan's came up with that. He was in the military and trained to use a variety of weapons, including RPGs. And in case you don't know what they are, RPGs are rocket-propelled grenades.

So, when Jonathan and his friend were discussing the fundamentals of their faith, the friend said, "Oh, this is like the weapons of our warfare." And he was right. We don't fight against flesh and blood, but against rulers and principalities (see Ephesians 6:12). We are in a battle, and just like Jonathan's buddy who prepared for a physical battle, we need to be prepared for a spiritual battle; otherwise, we'll be conquered.

We equip ourselves with RPGS: reading our Bibles, praying, going to church, and sharing our faith. These enable us to fight spiritual battles; they're the weapons of our warfare.

You need to hone these skills; you need to polish them. Like being in battle using a weapon to defend yourself—a sword, a gun, a knife—you need to hone these skills. It takes work, discipline, and action. You don't want to just "think about it" when it comes time to defend yourself or your family. You don't want to sit passively by when it comes time to take new ground. You want to be ready and capable.

We never outgrow these fundamentals. There is no checkbox after each one of these disciplines; they should be ongoing, something that we do each and every day.

Hold on to the progress you've made and keep moving forward. Keep your eyes on Jesus and invest in your marriage and family. Make the church your second home, your community, and build momentum for the next generation. Carry with you the weapons of your warfare, honing your skills, and putting them into practice. These are relationship goals that will outlive you, impacting many generations to come.

Prayer: Father, we pray for a personal revival today, that we would be rekindled in our love for You and Your Word. We want to be committed in our marriages and families like never before. We want to have a heart for people who don't know You. We want to be a part of the work that You're doing, and invest in it with all our hearts. Lord, some of us have drifted, and we need to return to You, our First Love. Help us step toward You in close fellowship and intimacy, like we used to do when we were brand-new believers. When it was a privilege and joy to open Your Word, and when we went to church with a sense of expectancy and anticipation. Remind us, Lord, to pray about everything, exercising the weapons of our warfare. Most of all, help us leave a legacy of faith—faith in Your Son, Jesus, the Way, the Truth, and the Life. In His name, amen.

QUESTIONS for Discussion

1. When David was on his deathbed, he told Solomon, "Know the God of your father, and serve Him with a loyal heart and with a willing mind; for the LORD searches all hearts and understands all the intent of the thoughts. If you seek Him, He will be found by you; but if you forsake Him, He will cast you off forever" (1 Chronicles 28:9 NKJV). Have you ever thought of what you might say on your deathbed, if given the chance? Why not share those words of wisdom now? Consider what message(s) you'd like to pass on to your children and grandchildren, and look for opportunities to share while you're still with them.

2. This chapter said, "The key is looking to Jesus, keeping your eyes on the Lord, because the devil wants you to take your eyes off of the Lord. He wants you to give up." In what ways are you sensing the enemy's pull to give up? How can you communicate this to your spouse and come together to speak truth over the lies? What changes might need to be made to keep your eyes on Jesus from this point forward?

3. Speaking directly to men, "Our family is our first responsibility before God and our most important mission field." Do you view your marriage and family as your number one priority after God? Does your work (or anything else) come first? How can you treat your family as your most important mission field?

4. Most fathers think it's the mother's responsibility to raise their children in the training and admonition of the Lord. Has this been your mindset as well? Where did this belief come from, and how can you work together to train up your children in the way they should go?

5. It was emphasized in this chapter that "modern families are being built on the foundation of Little League, the arts, education, or some other worldly success." As parents, how do you fall into this modern way of thinking? Are you so consumed with your children's potential that you are neglecting their spiritual foundation? What are some things you can implement into your family routine to build faith in Jesus and establish truth from God's Word?

6. "Kids are smart. They are watching you. They are observing how you handle real-life situations." Are you handling real-life situations in a healthy way? Do your children see you depending on God when things get tough? Do they see you investing in your relationship with Christ on a daily basis?

7. Reflect on Deuteronomy 6:1–2, which says, "These are the commands, decrees, and regulations that the LORD your God commanded me to teach you. You must obey them in the land you are about to enter and occupy, and you and your children and grandchildren must fear the LORD your God as long as you live. If you obey all his decrees and commands, you will enjoy a long life" (NLT). How is this passage foundational to your legacy? In what ways are you teaching (and living) in honor and reverence of God? What commands do you want your children to know and obey as they grow in their relationship with Christ?

8. From Psalm 127:1, we learn, "Unless the LORD builds a house, the work of the builders is wasted" (NLT). Has the Lord built your house? If not, will you allow Him to rebuild your foundation and strengthen your family through His Word? Remember, it's never too late!

9. Kids need a community of like-minded believers to help lead them. Are you trying to parent without the support of a Bible-believing,

healthy church environment? How could others pour into your children, enforcing what you're already teaching them?

10. "Growing together as a family doesn't mean you'll do everything perfectly. It doesn't mean you won't mess up, won't stumble." In light of Philippians 3:12–16, how can you get back up and keep going when you stumble? How can you live authentically so your children see progress over perfection?

11. We need to practice the weapons of our warfare, or RPGS:

Read your Bible

Pray

Go to church

Share your faith

Which of these disciplines needs more honing or practice in your life? How can these fundamentals strengthen your family and help you leave a lasting legacy?

CHAPTER 12

Personal Evangelism

*"But in your hearts revere Christ as Lord. Always be prepared
to give an answer to everyone who asks you to give the reason
for the hope that you have. But do this with gentleness
and respect." —1 Peter 3:15 (NIV)*

There is one thing believers and nonbelievers seem to have in common: They're both uptight about the gospel. Believers are uptight about sharing it, and nonbelievers are uptight about hearing it. But why is that?

Years ago, someone gave me four free tickets to Disneyland. We took our son, which left us with an extra ticket. I told my wife we shouldn't let it go to waste—we should give it away. She said we should just enjoy ourselves and not worry about it. But no, I had to give that ticket away. "After all," I thought, "how long will it take to get rid of a Disneyland ticket?"

Surprisingly, it took a long time. As I walked out of the park and approached random people, they just stared at me and my free ticket. I could practically read their minds: "What's the catch, buddy? What's your angle?" It took me more than half an hour to get rid of that ticket!

When sharing the gospel, people are often suspicious about the message we're sharing. They wonder what our angle is. And when they hear that there's a God in Heaven who loves them and is willing to forgive their sins, they think it's too good to be true. But even so, we should never be apprehensive or reluctant to talk about Jesus.

Let me put it this way: If you discovered the cure for cancer, would you keep it to yourself? Of course not! You'd want everyone to know. The gospel is even greater—it's the cure for the deepest problem we all face: sin. The solution? Jesus Christ.

Mark 16:15 says, "Go into all the world and preach the gospel to all creation" (NIV). Now, maybe the word "preach" makes you nervous. That's understandable. We tend to think of preaching in a negative way, as something bad. For example, if someone says something we don't like, we might say, "Hey, don't preach at me."

But in actuality, the Bible says preaching is a good thing. We don't have to do it loudly or forcefully; we can speak quietly and gently. We can whisper the gospel, share it conversationally, or even post it online. There are so many ways to share our faith. The key is to communicate it confidently without fear.

Romans 10:14 asks, "How can they call on him to save them unless they believe in him? And how can they believe in him if they have never heard about him? And how can they hear about him unless someone tells them?" (NLT).

The primary way people come to Jesus is through hearing the gospel. The Bible says, "Since God in his wisdom saw to it that the world would never know him through human wisdom, he has used our foolish preaching to save those who believe" (1 Corinthians 1:21 NLT).

God called Jonah to take the gospel to the city of Nineveh, which was filled with Israel's enemies. Jonah was reluctant and didn't go at first. But when he did go and preach the message God gave him, a great spiritual awakening broke out.

So, when you hear the words "preach the gospel" and feel reluctant, think of it this way: Go into all the world and *recommend* the Good News. After all, we recommend the best restaurants, the best movies, and the best songs. So why are we reluctant to recommend Jesus?

It's not as hard as you think. Simply go into your world, your sphere of influence, and share the best news they'll ever hear.

Meet Them Where They Are

The Great Commission isn't only for pastors—it's for businesspeople, students, stay-at-home moms, and you. Your mission field is what I like to call **FRAN**gelism: **F**riends, **R**elatives, **A**ssociates, and **N**eighbors. I bet you can think of at least one person who needs the gospel recommended to them. They might even be someone who is resistant to your faith.

It was President Lincoln who said, "The best way to destroy an enemy is to make him a friend." So, don't let other people's resistance intimidate you. Love them enough to reach out with the Good News—to friends and frenemies alike.

When I was a brand-new Christian at age 17, I heard a pastor say, "Go out and share your faith."

"Okay," I thought. "I'll take a stab at it."

Armed with a little booklet called "The Four Spiritual Laws" by Campus Crusade for Christ, I set out to find someone I could talk to. I found a middle-aged lady, walked up to her, and with my voice shaking, said, "Hi there, can I talk to you about God?"

Surprisingly, she said, "Yes, go ahead."

So, I sat down and literally began reading the booklet to her word for word: "This is called The Four Spiritual Laws, Copyright 1954, Campus Crusade for Christ. Law One: God loves you and has a wonderful plan for your life. Law Two: You're separated from Him by sin."

As I worked my way through the book, I thought: "This is not going to work. Why am I even doing this?"

Then I came to the page that asked, "Is there any good reason why you should not accept Jesus Christ right now?"

When I realized it was a question, I looked up.

She said, "No."

"Does that mean you want to accept Jesus Christ right now?" I asked.

She nodded her head and said, "Yes."

I had not planned for this kind of success, so I was really concerned about getting it right.

"Close your eyes," I said, "and let's just pray for a moment." (I had heard the pastor do this.)

As she kept her eyes closed, I frantically flipped through the booklet thinking, "What do I do now?"

Fortunately, I found a little prayer and led her through it.

After she was done praying, she opened her eyes and said, "Something just happened to me."

At that moment, I realized something had just happened to me too. I realized that God could use me—someone as unqualified as me—to share the gospel. I wasn't counting on being successful that day, but God used me, someone who knew so little, to lead someone to Christ. And if He can use me, He can use you.

Now, will your efforts always be successful? No, but that's okay.

A few weeks after I led that woman to Jesus, I ran into an old friend, Gregg (with two *g*'s). We used to hang out, and frankly, we had done a lot of drugs together.

After I became a Christian, I said to my friend Gregg, "Mark my words: Greg Laurie is never going to be a fanatic. You'll never see me walking down the street with a cross hanging around my neck, carrying a big Bible, and talking to people about God."

So, when I met Gregg on the street, he immediately saw the cross around my neck and the big Bible in my hand. We both burst out laughing. It was funny because I'd become the very person I said I wouldn't become.

When the laughter subsided, I said, "Gregg, I know what you're thinking: I've become a fanatic. But I have to tell you what Jesus has done for me."

"All right, Laurie," he said, "Go ahead, tell me."

So, I began telling him about Jesus, as much as I knew at that point.

But wouldn't you know, some random guy was eavesdropping on our conversation, and right in the middle of my testimony, he said, "I have a few questions for you, Christian."

I remember thinking, "Okay, what are they? I'm ready. I've been a Christian for four weeks. I know everything."

Then he hit me with several difficult questions. I don't remember what they were exactly, probably something along the lines of "How could a loving God allow suffering?" or "How could a God of love send people to Hell?"

Well, I didn't have the answers to those questions.

And to make matters worse, my friend Gregg joined in and said, "Yeah, Laurie, what about those questions?"

Needless to say, I was dumbfounded and went away embarrassed and ashamed.

But you know what? I determined that day that I was going to study the Bible and have answers to those questions in the future.

Scripture tells us: "Do your best to present yourself to God as one approved, a worker who does not need to be ashamed and who correctly handles the word of truth" (2 Timothy 2:15 NIV).

So yes, we need to be prepared. But even when you don't know the answers, you can still share what you do know: "I once was lost, but now I'm found." This is true for every Christian, and enough to start a conversation.

Tell Your Story

In Hawaii, there's an expression I like called "talk story." It's part of the island dialect often referred to as Pidgin English or Hawai'i Creole.

When someone says, "Let's talk story," they mean, "Let's catch up and enjoy a friendly conversation."

You might even hear it this way: "Hey, braddah, come talk story."

I love this phrase because I believe we should all "talk story."

Each of us has a unique story of how we came to faith in Christ, which includes the biblical story of the life, death, and resurrection of Jesus Christ. God has given us an evangelistic toolbox if you will, and one of the best tools in it is our personal testimony. This tool can be used as a bridge to share the gospel.

Listen, people can argue with your theology, and they can argue with the Bible, but they can't argue with your story. The greatest expert on you is you! Don't underestimate the power of your personal testimony.

In Revelation 12:11, we read about believers who overcame the devil "by the blood of the Lamb and by the word of their testimony" (NKJV). This tells us just how powerful our testimony is. A person cannot argue with you about what God has done in your life.

Now, your story doesn't need to be dramatic or inflated. In fact, you can start the conversation by saying, "Let me tell you how I used to live."

Using my testimony as an example, I've often shared about my lifestyle choices and the stupid things I did. I was living an empty life. But the day I heard someone on my high school campus sharing the gospel, everything changed. I specifically remember him sharing Jesus' words that went something like this: "You are either for me or against me." And that's what it took to open my eyes. My testimony might not be mind-blowing or fantastical, but it's my story.

Other people, however, have incredible testimonies to share. I've interviewed Michael Franzese, former member of the Colombo crime family. He was considered a "goodfella" and mafioso, but God got a hold of him while he was in solitary confinement, and he surrendered his life to Christ. He has a radical and impressive testimony.

I've also talked to Alice Cooper, rockstar extraordinaire, who was also an alcoholic and drug addict. But God got hold of him.

Alice never needed manufactured shock value. He lived the wild life. He walked through fame, addiction, and darkness—and survived. His testimony is powerful, surprising, and deeply moving.

You might not think your story is interesting enough. After all, you never broke the law, and you weren't addicted to anything but Ho Hos and Ding Dongs at the age of four. But listen, there's no need to make your past sound more interesting than your present. I've heard some people share the details of their life before they were Christians, and frankly, their old life sounded better than their new life. I've even heard people share their testimony on one occasion, but years later, share it again with new, exaggerated details.

Your story matters more than you think, but be careful not to boast about what you gave up for Christ. Boast about what He gave up for you.

"But Greg," you might say, "You have no idea what I left behind to follow Jesus."

My answer: You left nothing. You gave up nothing to follow Christ.

In the apostle Paul's words,

> "Yes, all the things I once thought were so important are gone from my life. Compared to the high privilege of knowing Christ Jesus as my Master, firsthand, everything I once thought I had going for me is insignificant—dog dung. I've dumped it all in the trash so I could embrace Christ and be embraced by him" (Philippians 3:8 MSG).

The New King James Version says it this way: "Yet indeed I also count all things loss for the excellence of the knowledge of Christ Jesus my Lord, for whom I have suffered the loss of all things, and count them as rubbish, that I may gain Christ."

In England, you might hear, "Oh that is rubbish, just rubbish."

But the word *rubbish* doesn't land the same way it did many decades ago. Even the word *garbage* doesn't communicate what Paul was saying. He called the things he once thought were so important *dog dung*, or poop.

"That is too graphic," you might say. "You shouldn't say the word 'poop.'"

Well, Paul said it in the Bible, so deal with it.

Here's an example to drive home this point: When you take your dog out for a walk and use one of those little blue bags to clean up his poop, you don't go home and show it to the family. You don't open the little bag and ask them to smell it. No. You tie it up, throw it in the dumpster, and shut the lid.

And this is exactly what you should do with your past. Don't be known for who you were; be known for who you are in Christ. Your story is more about Him, not you. So, share your testimony openly and honestly, but make sure it leads to the main story: the life, death, and resurrection of Jesus.

Use Language They Understand
One day, I was in a restaurant, and a lady recognized me.

She said, "Are you Greg Laurie?"

I said, "Yeah, I am."

She said, "Well, it's nice to meet you."

Then she gestured toward her husband, saying, "This is my husband; he's a heathen. Can you say something to help him believe in Jesus?"

The poor guy was just getting ready to take a bite of his hamburger when this happened. He froze mid-bite and looked at me like a deer caught in the headlights. I felt so bad for him.

I said, "Hey, man, enjoy your burger, okay? God bless you."

While there is a sense of urgency in sharing the gospel, discernment is needed. Don't embarrass a person. Don't make a scene. Don't create unnecessary friction.

Another problem I see in evangelism is the overuse of "Christianese," that cryptic language only Christians understand.

We start our conversations with these questions:

Have you been washed in the blood?

Have you been born again?

Have you been justified?

Do you belong to the body of Christ?

But what do these questions mean to the average person?

By telling people to get washed in blood, be born again, and become part of some "body," it's like we're speaking a foreign language.

I'm not saying we should never use biblical terminology, but we can't assume our listeners automatically understand these concepts. We need to be extra careful how we communicate the gospel.

Keep at It

Sometimes, we get tired of sharing the gospel, not because we don't care about people's salvation, but because we aren't sure it's working.

But listen, we need to keep at it even when we're weary or doubtful. As Paul says in Galatians 6:9, "So let's not get tired of doing what is good. At just the right time we will reap a harvest of blessing if we don't give up" (NLT).

Jesus displayed this kind of diligence when He ministered to the Samaritan woman at the well.

John 4:5–7 says,

> "Eventually he came to the Samaritan village of Sychar, near the field that Jacob gave to his son Joseph. Jacob's well was there; and Jesus, tired from the long walk, sat wearily beside the well about noontime. Soon a Samaritan woman came to draw water, and Jesus said to her, 'Please give me a drink'" (NLT).

He was tired, yet He still had time for this burned-out immoral woman. The Bible says we are to be on gospel duty at all times, but it's not in our own strength.

There are many times when I'm completely exhausted and a ministry opportunity comes my way. Honestly, I'm not always excited about these opportunities. Especially after a long day, I'm not always in the mood to get up and speak. But every time I step up to the plate and share the Word of God, He blesses it. And it's at those times that I've started on empty and ended on full.

Luke 6:38 says, "Give, and you will receive. Your gift will return to you in full—pressed down, shaken together to make room for more, running over, and poured into your lap. The amount you give will determine the amount you get back" (NLT).

What you give will be given back to you. Pressed down. Shaken together. Running over.

So, as I take the blessings God has given me, not hoarding them but sharing them, He replenishes my cup.

Interestingly, my wife accused me of being a hoarder the other day. We were cleaning out my office, and she said, "You really need to get rid of this."

"But," I answered thoughtfully, "you never know; I might need this in the future."

Her reply was, "You're becoming a hoarder."

The truth is, we can be hoarders with the gospel. We can keep it all to ourselves, but how selfish is that? The Lord fills our cup, and we think, "Okay, now I have my blessings. I'd better hold on tightly to them." But Luke tells us to share the blessings, to pour them out.

So, keep at it. Don't grow weary in doing good. God will fill you up again and again.

Let the Training Begin
Evangelism is a process.

First, you lead someone to Christ, and they cross the finish line. They are saved by grace through faith. Next, there's training to be done, spiritual disciplines to help them grow stronger.

It's sort of like starting a gym membership. Spiritually, the moment someone walks through the door, God sees them as completely fit and whole. But every Christian still needs regular exercise and personal training to mature in their faith.

Now, you might be surprised to learn that the term *Christian* is only mentioned three times in Scripture. It wasn't a title believers gave to themselves; it was actually a term used by nonbelievers to mock Jesus' followers.

Something similar happened in the 1960s and '70s when those who committed their lives to Christ were labeled, "Jesus Freaks." Back then, it wasn't meant to be a compliment, but today, some people might wear "Jesus Freak" as a badge of honor.

There is a term, however, that accurately describes every believer: disciple. It's mentioned more than 250 times in the Bible and applies to all of us. We are disciples of Jesus Christ, and we are called to disciple others. Neglecting this part of evangelism is detrimental to the church. We need discipleship to grow, mature, and lead others in faith.

Paul explained it best:

> Now these are the gifts Christ gave to the church: the apostles, the prophets, the evangelists, and the pastors and teachers. Their responsibility is to equip God's people to do his work and build up the church, the body of Christ. This will continue until we all come to such unity in our faith and knowledge of God's Son that we will be mature in the Lord, measuring up to the full and complete standard of Christ. Then we will no longer be immature like children. We won't be tossed and blown about by every wind of new teaching. We will not be influenced when people try to trick us with lies so clever they sound like the truth. Instead, we will speak the truth in love, growing in every way more and more like Christ, who is the head of his body, the church. (Ephesians 4:11–15 NLT)

It's Both Learning and Teaching

Discipleship means you're a learner who accepts instruction and makes it your rule of conduct. When you say "Jesus is Lord," you follow, study, and apply His teachings to your life. Jesus is our Master, Teacher, and Savior. We apply His teachings, His instructions, and His wisdom, not somebody else's. We are not following human opinions or what the world has to say.

That is why the apostle Paul said, "Imitate me, just as I also imitate Christ" (1 Corinthians 11:1 NKJV). Paul never stopped being a student of Jesus. He never stopped being a disciple. And we never stop being disciples of Jesus either.

> Jonathan's Story: I have a friend who owns a martial arts studio with his brother. They both love the Lord and often bring people from their academy to the church. One of the unique ways they teach martial arts is to come up with brand-new techniques that have not yet been taught. They instill these techniques along with the fundamentals, and encourage advanced students to "disciple" newcomers. On any given day, you'll see my friends overseeing the class, giving insight and correction, but allowing the advanced students to spar with newer students to help them improve.

This is a perfect picture of discipleship and what Jesus calls us to do. Exercising our faith by training others is how we mature in Christ. It's how we equip people to do His work and build up the church. But discipleship doesn't only happen inside a church building.

It's Making Disciples as We Go

When Jesus gave the command to "go and make disciples of all nations" (Matthew 28:19 NIV), the word *go* in this passage is rather interesting. I don't want to get too nerdy on you here, but there's an important insight I want to point out. The Greek word for *go* is a passive present participle.

Now, don't zone out on me. What this means is the emphasis in Greek is not on the word *go* as the action, but more on the word *make*. In other words, Jesus' command could be translated, "While you are going, make disciples."

While you are being a teacher in the classroom, make disciples.

While you're being a student at the university, make disciples.

While you are being a parent in the home, make disciples.

While you are being a lawyer in the workplace, make disciples.

Evangelism happens every day. It isn't reserved just for missionaries overseas. It really comes down to what Moses said in Deuteronomy 6:5–7:

> "You shall love the LORD your God with all your heart, with all your soul, and with all your strength. And these words which I command you today shall be in your heart. You shall teach them diligently to your children, and shall talk of them when you sit in your house, when you walk by the way, when you lie down, and when you rise up" (NKJV).

This is our mission. As we go along in life, we look for opportunities to share the gospel and encourage believers in their faith.

Living Among Unbelievers

Before Jesus ascended to Heaven, He said, "You will be my witnesses in Jerusalem, and in all Judea and Samaria, and to the ends of the earth" (Acts 1:8 NIV). These were very specific instructions for the believers in the first century. Jerusalem was ground zero for them. That's where they were at the time Jesus gave the commission.

We, too, have our own Jerusalem, Judea, Samaria, and the ends of the earth.

Jerusalem is our immediate inner circle. These are the people we can call at any time. They're the ones we see on a regular basis, and the ones we're most likely to share our faith with. In fact, those in our inner circle are likely believers, but even if they're not, we feel comfortable enough to talk about Jesus.

Then there's Judea. These are extended family members and friends. Every time you see them, you pick up where you left off. They're not as close as your inner circle, but you still find opportunities to share with them. And you know what? It doesn't need to be awkward.

You can say something as simple as, "I don't know if I told you, but I put my faith in Jesus. It's given me a whole new perspective, and I just have to tell you about it."

Chances are the people in your "Judea" are going to listen. They're going to care enough about your life-changing experience to say, "That's great. Let's grab a cup of coffee and talk about it."

This brings us to our third area of influence: Samaria. Our Samaria is typically outside our comfort zone. Historically speaking, Samaritans were half-Jew, half-Gentile, and the relationship between Jews and Samaritans was icy at best.

For us, these are people we don't necessarily get along with, yet we still share something in common with them. Maybe they have a heart for the homeless, or are empathetic toward something you're passionate about. Whatever common ground you have is a bridge you can build upon. You don't need to feel intimidated by your "Samaria," but rather, find common ground for the sake of Christ.

This leaves us with our final commission: the ends of the earth. These are the places we don't want to go. We don't know these people, we might not like them, and we might even be fearful of what this requires. Yet God calls us to go anyway.

The ends of the earth are the last people on your list: the next-door neighbor who called the cops on you because you left your trash cans out overnight. The person who had your car towed because it was parked in front of their house for an hour. Yes, Jesus commands us to preach the gospel even to the outermost people on our list.

Living among unbelievers isn't easy, and we won't always be successful. But God isn't looking for success. When we see Jesus face to face, He's not going to say, "Well done, good and successful servant." Instead, He's going to say, "Well done, good and faithful servant!" (Matthew 25:23 NIV).

Evangelism is part of faith. It's not optional or arbitrary; it's a divine calling for every Christian. Most importantly, it's the opportunity to share the best news anyone could ever hear.

Prayer: Lord, we need the boldness of Your Spirit to reach the lost. People everywhere are in desperate need of the Savior. Thank You for equipping us to step out in faith and share the Good News with everyone in our circle of influence. Please remove doubt and fear, replacing them with confidence in who You are and what You've done. Give us opportunities to share our story, and let our testimony be a bridge to the greatest story of all. Help us faith-

fully carry out the Great Commission: "Go into all the world and preach the Good News to everyone" (Mark 16:15 NLT). In Jesus' name, amen.

QUESTIONS for Discussion

1. There's one thing believers and nonbelievers have in common: They are both uptight about the gospel. Believers are uptight about sharing it, and nonbelievers are uptight about hearing it. What are some valid reasons believers are hesitant to share their faith today? What cultural factors play into the resistance?

2. Mark 16:15 says, "Go into all the world and preach the gospel to all creation" (NIV). The word *preach* makes many people nervous. Especially if they're not good at communicating, they might feel ill-equipped to share the gospel. What are some simple ways to share the gospel without being "preachy"?

3. FRANgelism stands for Friends, Relatives, Associates, and Neighbors. Reflect on this and think of those within your circle who need to hear the gospel. How does "FRANgelism" help reframe your mission field?

4. God has given us an evangelistic toolbox, and one of the best tools in it is our personal testimony. This tool can be used as a bridge to share the gospel. If you were asked to share your testimony today, would you be prepared? How can your story help someone else recognize their need for Christ? Remember: Your testimony doesn't need to be dramatic or inflated to make a difference.

5. This chapter warns us not to boast about what we gave up for Christ, but what He gave up for us. Are you tempted to boast about your past life and the things you gave up to follow Jesus? How can a shift in perspective help you focus on what He gave up for you? See Galatians 1:4–5, Galatians 2:20, 1 Peter 3:18.

6. While there is a sense of urgency in sharing the gospel, discernment is needed. We shouldn't embarrass people, make a scene, or cause unnecessary friction. Have you ever had a negative experience in evan-

gelism? What were some of the tactics used? How could it have been done more effectively, in love, wisdom, and discernment?

7. This chapter reveals another problem in evangelism: the overuse of Christianese, which includes terminology only Christians understand. What are some common phrases Christians use without thinking? How can important biblical concepts be communicated clearly without the use of Christianese?

8. Sometimes, we get tired of sharing the gospel, not because we don't care about people's salvation, but because we aren't sure it's working. What is the answer to this problem according to Galatian 6:9? Reflect on times when you've grown "weary in doing good." How did you get out of that slump?

9. When we become Christians, God sees us as completely fit and whole, but we still need regular exercise and personal training to help us grow stronger in our faith. Who are the "personal trainers" in your life? How do they encourage you to exercise your faith? When discipling others, what are specific things that ought to be taught?

10. Deuteronomy 6:5–7 says, "You shall love the LORD your God with all your heart, with all your soul, and with all your strength. And these words which I command you today shall be in your heart. You shall teach them diligently to your children, and shall talk of them when you sit in your house, when you walk by the way, when you lie down, and when you rise up" (NKJV). Reflect on this passage as a starting point for evangelism. In what God-given roles are you making disciples as you go?

11. This chapter mentions four different regions as our mission field: Jerusalem, Judea, Samaria, and the ends of the earth. Which "region" makes you most uncomfortable, and why? What were some of the tips given in this chapter for evangelizing even the most difficult people?

12. Living among unbelievers isn't easy, and we won't always be successful. But God isn't looking for success. When sharing the gospel, what is more important to the Lord than success? How does this encourage you to be faithful, trusting God with the outcome?

CHAPTER 13

Relationship Goals That Last Forever

"He has made everything beautiful in its time. Also, he has put eternity into man's heart, yet so that he cannot find out what God has done from the beginning to the end." —Ecclesiastes 3:11 (ESV)

Somehow, I managed to go 72 years without ever having to go to the hospital for any kind of surgery. When it came time for my hip to be replaced, I put it off for a long, long time. I knew it needed to be done, but I kept postponing and postponing. However, the pain got worse and worse until it was hard to walk. And then I had a cane. That's when I decided, "Okay, I'm just gonna do this."

When I got to the hospital, they wheeled me down to where I was going to have the surgery. I was lying there on the little gurney, looking up at the lights as I went by. I've watched this scene in so many TV shows. I was like, "Here we go."

Then I arrived in a giant room, with super bright lights and all kinds of frightening tools on the tables. In case you didn't know, hip replacement surgery is a crazy procedure. They use a big titanium rod that connects to a little silicone socket, and with a mallet, they pound that baby in (a mallet, for heaven's sake!). Trust me, you do not want to be awake for this.

When I woke up, I didn't know where I was. I didn't know what had happened. Then a nurse asked, "Are you hungry?"

Despite the fact that I was still under heavy anesthesia, I said, "Yes, I'm hungry." Then she said, "Would you like a turkey sandwich or a peanut butter sandwich?" And even in my deranged state, I thought, "How good could hospital turkey be?"

In the days to follow, there were certain protocols I had to follow, including using a walker, which I did not enjoy at all. Eventually, I made my way to a cane, and ultimately, I was able to walk on my own two feet again. So, really, it was all about getting my balance back, and effectively learning how to walk all over again.

That's life, isn't it? We start out as little babies crawling, then we take our first steps, and then we begin to walk on our own. The older we get, the more independent we become. And then we get a lot older, need a hip replacement, and end up falling down and calling Life Alert. "I've fallen, and I can't get up!"

It's interesting to me how often the Bible compares the Christian life to a walk. It's not only learning how to walk, but how to walk with balance. And I think balance is so important in life. This is why 1 Timothy 4:8 says, "For physical training is of some value, but godliness has value for all things, holding promise for both the present life and the life to come" (NIV).

While there's some value in physical training, there's eternal value in godly training. And that's where the right balance comes in. That's where our priorities are aligned. That's where our temporary goals become "forever" goals.

Setting "Forever" Goals on Three Principles

As Christians, we exist for three purposes:

The glorification of God

The edification of the saints

The evangelization of the world

What do you think someone on the street would say if you asked them, "Why do you exist? Why are you here on this planet? What is the meaning of your life?"

You'd probably hear all sorts of answers such as, "I'm here to be happy. I'm here to live out my truth. I'm here to follow my passions." But that is not what the Bible teaches. It's not that God doesn't want you to be happy, in fact, He does. But you must go about it in the right way. So, we find out why we exist on earth from something that is actually said in Heaven.

Revelation 4:11 says, "You are worthy, O Lord, to receive glory and honor and power; for You created all things, and by Your will they exist and were created" (NKJV).

So, why do we exist? Simple answer: to glorify God. It is for God's pleasure that we exist and were created. As Ephesians 1:4–6 says,

> "Even before he made the world, God loved us and chose us in Christ to be holy and without fault in his eyes. God decided in advance to adopt us into his own family by bringing us to himself through Jesus Christ. This is what he wanted to do, and it gave him great pleasure. So we praise God for the glorious grace he has poured out on us who belong to his dear Son" (NLT).

If you really want relationships that last, you will step into your purpose—your existence—with the ultimate goal of glorifying God. No more wasting your life on the pursuit of "nothingness." Instead, you'll pursue your heavenly calling, your heavenly citizenship, while still living on this earth.

Remember Philippians 3:20–21 where Paul says, "But we are citizens of heaven, where the Lord Jesus Christ lives. And we are eagerly waiting for him to return as our Savior. He will take our weak mortal bodies and change them into glorious bodies like his own, using the same power with which he will bring everything under his control" (NLT).

As citizens of Heaven, we should know what the culture of Heaven is like, and we should be not waiting until we get to Heaven to live that way. We should be living that way here on earth first. So, let's look at each of the three principles on which we can build forever goals.

1. Glorifying God

C. H. Spurgeon said once in a sermon, "To glorify God, that is the business of our lives."

We aren't here to achieve career success, financial security, or fame. We aren't here to follow our passions, make ourselves happy, or live out our truth (whatever that means). Your life is a gift from God, so live it for Him.

One of the ways you can glorify God is through worship. And worship isn't only about singing songs or playing on harps; it's about a heart posture before God, exalting Him above all things. We're going to worship for eternity in Heaven, so we need to be doing it here on earth. After all, this life is preparation for eternity.

God has specifically designed relationships that last forever to focus on eternity more than they focus on the here and now. As Colossians 3:2-4 reminds us, "Set your mind on things above, not on things on the earth. For you died, and your life is hidden with Christ in God. When Christ who is our life appears, then you also will appear with Him in glory" (NKJV).

We are here for the glorification of God. And what does that mean? It means to live for Christ. Are you living for Christ in your singleness, dating, marriage, and parenting? Are you living for Christ as you age, need hip replacements, and learn to walk again?

2. Edifying the saints

Next in line, we're here for the edification of the saints. In other words, we're to be an active part of the church and realize it's not about me, it's about *we*.

We are a family.

We need each other.

This is important in today's culture where so many are turning to artificial intelligence (AI) for actual companionship instead of having human interaction. We need God and we need people.

Studies have been done that have revealed countless health benefits from actually attending church and being part of a community. Harvard School of Public Health found that people who attend church at least once a week live longer, experience less depression, and have stronger social support networks. Other studies have shown that worship actually calms the nervous system and prayer reduces stress. Isn't that interesting? Now these are scientific studies that are effectively catching up with Scripture, because we are wired for worship and relationship. God built us for connection with Him and with each other.

I was talking the other day with a psychologist who happens to treat affluent people. And I said, "Tell me the top things that people need help with."

His answer? "The number one thing people need help with is emptiness."

I found this very fascinating. Then he shared another thing people are struggling with: a lack of connectivity. People are withdrawn. They're not connecting to other people. But the answers to these problems is simple: They need God, and they need the church. It could change everything, right?

By God's grace, He has given us different gifts for edification. So, if He has given you the ability to prophesy, speak out with as much faith as God has given you. If your gift is serving others, serve them well. If you're a teacher, teach well. If your gift is to encourage others, let your words be encouraging. If it is giving, give generously. If God has given you a leadership ability, take that responsibility seriously. And if you have a gift for showing kindness, do it gladly. Don't just pretend. Love people with your gifts. Edify the saints, the body of Christ. We need what you have to offer!

3. Evangelizing the world

The third purpose we were created for is evangelizing the world. This is not only because the world needs to hear the gospel, but because it's actually life-giving to us as well.

In Acts chapter 2, we read about the Day of Pentecost, when the Holy Spirit was poured out and the gospel was preached. Verse 41 says, "Those who believed what Peter said were baptized and added to the church that day—about 3,000 in all" (NLT).

This is what the early church spent their time doing, and this is what we should be spending our time doing today. Many couples or families who go on mission trips together come back with a whole new perspective. Their once-narrow view is expanded once they've experienced the gospel's power firsthand. But listen, evangelizing the world first starts in your home. It begins with your family, your neighborhood, and your community, and spreads from there.

Setting a goal to reach the lost for Christ is one of the most important goals you could set. Evangelism builds faith, strengthens marriages, and sets an example for the next generation. And I believe it can be healing for hurting marriages, by turning self-centeredness into Christ-centeredness.

Longing for God Himself

Little girls grow up wanting to be princesses; they long for a prince to come rescue them. And boys grow up with the romantic notion of meeting some beautiful girl who will meet the deepest needs of their life. We long for someone to complete us, to be with us, to understand us, to fulfill us, and to bring significance to our lives.

In the movie *Shall We Dance?*, one of the characters expressed it like this:

> We need a witness to our lives. There's a billion people on the planet. . . . I mean, what does anyone's life really mean? But in a marriage, you're promising to care about everything. The good things, the bad things, the terrible things, the mundane things—all of it, all of the time, every day. You're saying, "Your life will not go unnoticed, because I will notice it. Your life will not go unwitnessed, because I will be your witness."

God, in His kindness to humanity, gave men and women to each other to comfort us, help us, and fulfill us, and we praise Him for that. Apart from Jesus Christ Himself, my wife is the most wonderful gift God has ever given me. But deep down, at the very core of our souls, beyond any other human longing, what you and I really long for is God Himself.

The primary longing of every human being (whether they realize it or not) is to walk with God, know His voice, love Him, and be loved by Him. The Westminster Catechism says, "Man's chief end is to glorify God and enjoy him forever." That is the most satisfying and fulfilling thing we can do as human beings.

Yes, a man can sometimes please and fulfill a woman, and a woman can sometimes fulfill a man. But a man can't do everything or be everything for a woman, and a woman can't do everything or be everything for a man.

In some pop music, a guy or girl will sing "you are my world" or "you are my everything." It sounds romantic and sweet and all that, but God never intended one man or one woman to fill up all the empty places in our soul. No one person can do that. No one person should ever be expected to do that—no one but God alone.

Someone has well said, "Never expect man to do for you what only God can do. And don't confuse the two!"

Our Father in Heaven is the One we really long for. Jesus is the wonderful Prince who has come to rescue us, and will come again to receive us to Himself. The Holy Spirit is the One who will be with us through all of life, "closer than hands or feet, closer than breathing."[25]

He will be that witness that our hearts long for. He will fill the empty days and the lonely moments with His own presence and nearness and wisdom and conversation and cheer. We were created to know God. And whether we are married, single, divorced, or widowed, He will be our Companion and Friend and Defender, and help us to become all we were created to be.

Life with Christ begins when you admit you are a sinner, and you cry out to Him, asking for His help and His forgiveness. Then Christ Himself will come and live inside of you, and give you the strength to be the man or the woman God has called you to be, whatever your marital status. But if you are married, He will enable you to become the husband your wife dreams of, or the wife your husband longs for. There is no sin He can't forgive, no obstacle He can't overcome, and no empty place He can't fill.

New life begins today, as you look to Him and say, "Lord, I need You."

Prayer: Lord, how we need You in every way. We have fallen short in our relationships, and we need You to revive us again. Thank You for Your grace, Your forgiveness, and Your restoration. Thank You for Your Son, Jesus, who rescues us from sin and death. We praise You for sending Your Spirit to live in us, giving us the strength needed to navigate this life. You desire a close relationship with us, and deep down, we desire to be in fellowship with You. Even though we fall short time and time again, You are not mad at us; You are mad about us. We love You, Lord, and commit every relationship goal to You, now and forever. In the holy and mighty name of Jesus, amen.

QUESTIONS for Discussion

1. This comparison is made: "we start out as little babies crawling, then we take our first steps, and then we begin to walk on our own." Looking back on your own journey, how did you follow this pattern of crawling, taking baby steps, and then walking with Jesus? Are you still trying to find your balance?

2. There are three purposes for mankind: Glorifying God, edifying the saints, and evangelizing the world. How are these principles the backbone of every personal and relationship goal? How can you align your life, marriage, and family with these core principles?

3. In Philippians 3:20–21, Paul says, "But we are citizens of heaven, where the Lord Jesus Christ lives. And we are eagerly waiting for him to return as our Savior. He will take our weak mortal bodies and change them into glorious bodies like his own, using the same power with which he will bring everything under his control" (NLT). As citizens of Heaven, how should we be living now? Are there any areas where you are more focused on the world rather than Heaven?

4. "We're to be an active part of the church, and realize it's not just about me, it's about *we*." How has your connectedness to the body of Christ been edifying to you? How are you edifying other believers? If you're not currently attending church, what is holding you back?

5. So many in today's culture are turning to AI for actual companionship instead of engaging in human interaction. People's number one issue is emptiness. Do you believe AI (and the internet in general) gives people a false sense of connectivity? How has this played out in your life? What is the solution for the emptiness people feel?

6. When you hear the word *evangelism*, do you automatically think about mission trips and world travel? What about evangelism in your own home, with your own family? How could a heart for the lost strengthen your marriage and lead your children by example?

7. Reflect on this foundational truth: "Deep down, at the very core of our souls, beyond any other human longing, what you and I really long for is God Himself." What longings did you have growing up that you eventually realized could only be fulfilled in Christ? What about now? Are there current longings you're struggling to align with God's purpose?

8. The Westminster Catechism says, "Man's chief end is to glorify God and enjoy him forever." Greg said, "That is the most satisfying and fulfilling thing we can do as human beings." How can every relationship goal start by glorifying God? What could this mean for your faith, marriage, family, and witness for Christ?

9. The Lord's intimacy in our lives is described like this: "He will be that witness that our hearts long for. He will fill the empty days and the lonely moments with His own presence and nearness and wisdom and conversation and cheer." How has God been the witness your heart longs for? In what specific ways has He filled empty, lonely moments with His presence?

10. This chapter reminds us that God "will enable you to become the husband your wife dreams of, or the wife your husband longs for. There is no sin He can't forgive, no obstacle He can't overcome, and no empty place He can't fill." How is this true in your own life? Are you the husband or wife God enables you to be? In every relationship, every goal, and every moment, repeat the words, "Lord, I need you."

ENDNOTES

1 Westrick-Payne, Krista K. "Marriage-Divorce Ratio in the U.S.: Geographic Variation, 2025." Accessed at: https://www.bgsu.edu/ncfmr/resources/data/family-profiles/FP-24-27.html.

2 Aragao, Carolina, et al. "The Modern American Family." Accessed at: https://www.pewresearch.org/social-trends/2023/09/14/the-modern-american-family/.

3 Phares, Emily. "Dating Statistics and Facts." Accessed at: https://www.forbes.com/health/dating/dating-statistics/.

4 Mayol-Garcia, Yeris. "Number, Timing, and Duration of Marriages and Divorces: 2016." Accessed at: https://www.census.gov/library/publications/2021/demo/p70-167.html.

5 Dobson, James. *Love for a Lifetime* (Multnomah Books, 2004).

6 Barclay, William. *The Letters of James and Peter* (Louisville: Westminster John Knox Press, 2003), page 251.

7 Hopcke, Robert H. and Paul A. Schwartz. *Little Flowers of Francis of Assisi* (Boston: New Seeds Books, 2006), page 3.

8 Swindoll, Charles R. *Growing Strong in the Seasons of Life* (Grand Rapids: Zondervan, 1983), page 60.

9 Love, Patricia and Steven Stosny. *How to Improve Your Marriage Without Talking About It* (New York: Broadway, 2007), page 49.

10 *Ibid.*

11 Vaughan, Peggy. *The Monogamy Myth* (New York: Newmarket Press, 2003), page 7.

12 "The Odds Are Against You." *Spy. The New York Monthly.* March, 1987, page 47.

13 Johnson, Alan F. *1 Corinthians* (Downers Grove: InterVarsity, 2004), page 17.

14 All "duty" quotes can be accessed at: http://www. worldofquotes.com/topic/Duty/1/index.html.

15 Accessed at: http://www.worldofquotes.com/author/ Mark+Twain/12/index.html.

16 Chesterton, G. K. *The Everlasting Man* (Hodder & Stoughton, 1925).

17 Henry, Matthew. *Matthew Henry's Commentary on the Whole Bible* (Peabody Hendrickson, 1996), Genesis 2:21.

18 Wiersbe, Warren. *The Wiersbe Bible Commentary: New Testament* (Colorado Springs: David C. Cook, 2007), page 56.

19 Pope John Paul II. *A Pilgrim Pope: Messages for the World* (Kansas City: McMeel, 1999), page 318.

20 Wallerstein, Judith S. and Sandra Blakeslee. *Second Chances* (New York: Houghton Mifflin, 1996).

21 Accessed at: http://www.enduringword.com/commentaries/4019.htm.

22 Weitzman, Lenore J. *The Divorce Revolution* (Glencoe: Free Press, 1985).

23 Kantrowitz, Barbara. "Breaking the Divorce Cycle." *Newsweek*. January 13, 1992.

24 Merritt, James. *What God Wants Every Dad to Know: The Most Important Principles You Can Teach Your Child* (Harvest House Publishers, 2013).

25 Jeremiah, David. *God in You* (Multnomah Publishers, 1998), page 102.

OTHER WORKS BY
GREG LAURIE

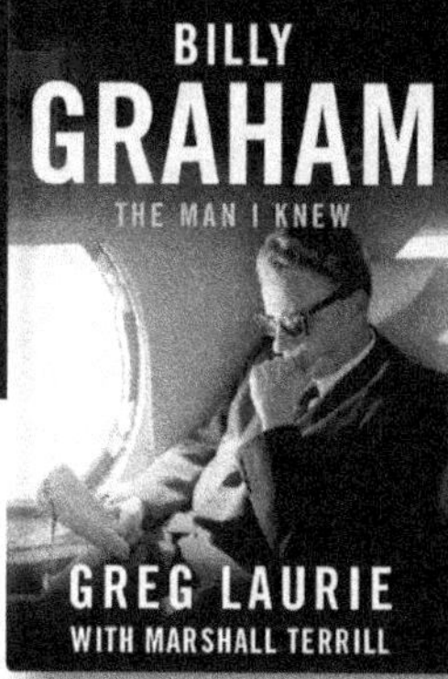

THIS APP INCLUDES FREE ACCESS TO POPULAR TITLES LIKE:

DOWNLOAD HARVEST+ TODAY!

ROKU SAMSUNG

harvest.org

Stream exclusive and never-before-seen content from Pastor Greg Laurie and Harvest Ministries on the Harvest+ app!

GREG LAURIE
show

FOLLOW TODAY!

discipleship

**Connect with the
Harvest: Discipleship Platform
to fellowship with likeminded believers
and find valuable resources.**

Grow with us at:
DISCIPLE.HARVEST.ORG